VISIONS
IN THE NIGHT

VISIONS
IN THE NIGHT

DREAMS FROM GOD TO INSTRUCT,
ENCOURAGE, GUIDE, AND BLESS

RUTH McMILLAN MAYFIELD

TATE PUBLISHING & *Enterprises*

Visions in the Night
Copyright © 2008 by Ruth McMillan Mayfield. All rights reserved.

This title is also available as a Tate Out Loud product. Visit www.tatepublishing.com for more information.

No part of this publication may be reproduced, stored in a retrieval system or transmitted in any way by any means, electronic, mechanical, photocopy, recording or otherwise without the prior permission of the author except as provided by USA copyright law.

All Scripture quotations are taken from the Holy Bible, King James Version, Cambridge, 1769. Used by permission. All rights reserved.

The opinions expressed by the author are not necessarily those of Tate Publishing, LLC.

Published by Tate Publishing & Enterprises, LLC
127 E. Trade Center Terrace | Mustang, Oklahoma 73064 USA
1.888.361.9473 | www.tatepublishing.com

Tate Publishing is committed to excellence in the publishing industry. The company reflects the philosophy established by the founders, based on Psalms 68:11,
"The Lord gave the word and great was the company of those who published it."

Book design copyright © 2008 by Tate Publishing, LLC. All rights reserved.
Cover design by Jacob Crissup
Interior design by Janae J. Glass

Published in the United States of America

ISBN: 978-1-60604-154-3
1. Inspirational: Motivational: Biography & Autobiography
2. Body, Mind & Spirit: Dreams
08.05.07

Now a thing was secretly brought to me, and mine ear received a little thereof. In thoughts from the visions of the night, when deep sleep falleth on men...

Job 4:13

And it shall come to pass afterward, that I will pour out my spirit upon all flesh; and your sons and your daughters shall prophesy, your old men shall dream dreams, your young men shall see visions: And also upon the servants and upon the handmaids in those days will I pour out my spirit.

Joel 2:28, 29

Table of Contents

Introduction	11
The Lord He is God	15
He is the Lord of Hosts	49
The Abundant Life	81
Overcoming Faith	119
Deep Calls unto Deep	153
Living in the Supernatural	183
Fulfilling my Destiny	217
Dream Interpretation and References	231
Index of Dream Categories	243

Trust in the LORD with all thine heart; and lean not unto thine own *understanding*. In all thy ways acknowledge him, and he shall direct thy paths.

Proverbs 3:5, 6

Introduction

This book is written for people who would like to gain a glimpse of how our loving God speaks to us in visions in the night to teach, prophesy, and bless (Genesis 46:2, Job 4:13, Daniel 7:7, 13). God has been giving me dreams for over thirty-five years. These dreams began as God delivered me from the nightmares that plagued my childhood. Some are prophetic; some are divine object lessons; some are typical of God speaking to us about ourselves. I pray that you are blessed and encouraged to seek the Lord, allowing Him to speak to you through His Word, the Bible. Then also expect Him to speak to you through people, nature, circumstances, and even dreams and visions.

The Lord recently used a series of events to bring the dreams of my past back into the center of my thoughts. I believe the Lord has brought forth these dreams that have been in a prophetic incubation for this kairos time. There were many more, but I have chosen those that had significant spiritual meaning to me, to include here.

The dreams are listed in chronological order, beginning in October 1972. They are grouped by chapter headings reflecting my spiritual maturity level and walk. This ordering is meant to show both a progressive revelation and maturing in the Lord. All dreams are categorized and indexed for quick reference.

There are some gaps in the dates. Usually because of an event in my life, good or tragic, that caused me not to dream as much. The complete testimony of my life is amazing, although long and complicated. It is incomplete without these dreams, which the Lord has used to shape my spiritual personality.

The dreams begin in October 1972. I accepted Jesus as my Savior, in late September 1972, reading a Gideon's Bible from a High School library. In April 1979, I first attended a church. I was baptized that August, and received an overflowing fullness of the Holy Spirit and began speaking in tongues in late September 1979. By this time I had read the entire Bible through a few times, most frequently Psalms, Job and the New Testament. In 1981, I began reading the Bible through chronologically every year, plus word and topic studies, and lots more Psalms and Proverbs. I continue to read it through at least every year or two, plus a lot of study. The Word of God is my favorite book!

All prophecy and teaching must be measured against the Word of God. Only two people in the Bible are named as having a gift for interpreting dreams, Joseph and Daniel. I do not claim to be an expert on dream interpretation. There are a few references at the back of this book, but there are no Josephs or Daniels today to help us interpret. We all have the Holy Spirit to help us though. In the comments, which accompany these dreams, I try to share how the Lord was, and is, speaking to me personally. I pray that my insight will bless you with insight of your own and cause greater awareness in you, that our Heavenly Father is speaking to you, everyday.

> Grow in grace, and in the knowledge of our Lord and Saviour Jesus Christ. To him be glory both now and forever. Amen.
>
> 2 Peter 3:18

The Lord He is God

Ball of Glory Fire

October 1972: vision of God

I found myself walking along a dirt road, rather a driveway, with buildings on either side. Off toward the distance, was a curved path lined with mature trees making a shady, inviting entrance to the area. As my eyes looked past the curve and down the path, I suddenly saw a ball of fire coming up the path. I stared for a moment, never having seen anything like it. It was about the size of a beach ball floating about six feet above the ground directly above the path headed in my direction.

I panicked. I ran into the building to my left, the closest one, to hide. The building was dorm style, like you would see at a camp in the woods, but not rustic. It had high windows, too high to see out of, or in, but they would let in air and light. There were cots lined along both sides of the room and about four or five people were inside chatting. I warned them that this ball of fire was coming toward us, but they didn't understand and didn't seem concerned. I knew it was getting close—I could feel it. One of the people was an older lady, I recognized her from my mother's restaurant job. She was a difficult, cross person most of the time. I thought because of her, the others wouldn't listen to me. Suddenly the ball of fire entered the room right through one of the windows at the far end. The window was closed, but it didn't cause any damage as it passed through. Again, this ball of fire was coming up the isle between the beds directly at me—only twenty feet away.

Nowhere to run! No time! I dove under the nearest cot. Now cots are generally quite close to the floor, and even though I was a rather thin person, the only part of me that would fit was my head and upper torso. I closed my eyes tight and held my hands over my eyes and ears at the same time to block out what I could of the impending devastation that would happen to those unassuming people. Perhaps it wouldn't even see me down here on the floor. They were just sitting on the beds. Even with my eyes facing the floor, tightly shut, and my hands over them—I could still see in my mind's eye this ball of fire coming toward me. It ignored the others and stopped for a moment, hovering directly above me.

Suddenly a flash of flame, like a laser, shot out of the ball of fire directly at the exposed portion of my lower back. I felt the searing etching like a tattoo as words were written on my flesh. It felt like a laser but with no burning pain. At the same time, I could see as if from above, though my face was under the cot toward the floor. I saw—I felt—the words *Jesus was here*. As the words were completed, I awoke with a start! I was lying on my stomach on my bed in my bedroom. I could feel the fresh burn on my flesh. I was afraid to move, so I lay for a long time thinking about what I had just experienced.

I knew that I had just seen God in a different form than I ever heard of or expected. I had thought myself better than the people in that room, yet they weren't afraid. I had been afraid and hadn't recognized God. Yet He had marked me. It felt wonderful to belong to God, yet fearful that I had been in His Presence and unexpectedly—I was still alive! When I finally got the courage to move, I was almost afraid to look in the mirror to see if there was anything there. It felt as if there was. *How would I ever explain how it got there? Who would believe it?* But there was nothing there when I looked in the mirror. I could still feel it as I went downstairs with the family to watch TV. Everyone—everything—looked normal, but for me, my world had forever changed.

Comment: This was the very first dream that I had from the Lord. I remember it clearly, as happens with life changing events—each detail is permanently cast in your memory. The dream originally occurred in October 1972 only one month after I made a decision to follow Jesus through reading a Gideon's Bible. I had fallen asleep after supper bored, a typical high school student.

I had not had any exposure to the Gospel prior to reading the Bible. I had at this time very little understanding of the handful of chapters of the New Testament I had read. No one I knew was a Christian. I was ashamed that I hadn't recognized God. I was determined to get to know Him so that would never happen again, yet I understood that He was so big that I could never assume I *could* recognize Him. *I belonged to God*, although I had no idea what that meant, I would always seek Him and His answers for every encounter in the future.

The Battle

December 1972: spiritual warfare

I was standing in a very large field, a menacing storm approaching. I ran toward a huge tree in the center of the field. As I approached the tree, a powerful bolt of lightning hit the ground close by. I stopped by the edge of the tree line, afraid to go under it because it might attract the lightning. The rain began falling in giant droplets soaking me instantly. There was no place for shelter, so I fell to my knees in the tall grass not knowing what to do. Looking up, I saw a huge silver horse that was arguing with the tree because it wanted to take shelter under the protesting branches. I was even more afraid of the tree and the horse than the storm, so I just lay there hoping they wouldn't notice me. Then I woke up.

Comment: This was a very short but disturbing dream. When I first dreamed this, I didn't understand it. I sensed good and evil, but I wasn't able to clearly discern which was which because both were supernatural. Later I understood the tree represents a powerful, prosperous evil kingdom. The silver horse represents God's wisdom and redemption coming as a swift, supernatural patrol to war against the evil on my behalf. The storm and lightning spoke of God's judgment of the evil and a shifting and installation of God's power and anointing in my life. The rain was God's blessing to ease the spiritual draught and cause Spiritual growth in my life. My natural tendency was to take refuge from the drenching rain under the huge tree, but the lightning made me see the tree as dangerous.

In these early days of my Salvation experience, I had no idea of the evil spiritual and generational hindrances in my background. I quickly learned about spiritual warfare because I found myself in a battle. God had sovereignly saved me, and the devil was not happy about it. Satan showed his hatred for me in many ways. So, on this day long ago, the Lord won the battle for my spiritual life and "Knighted" me into His Kingdom, equipping me for victory in every battle that would ever befall me.

House in New Jersey

April 1973: houses

I found myself wandering through a wonderful, warm, and friendly house. It had wooden floors and staircases. The doorways and windows were also wooden framed French style in a seasoned, dark stain. There were two or three staircases in this three-story house. Looking out the windows from the top floor and peering through the thick tree branches in the yard, you could hardly see the lush green grass and gardens below. The bottom floor had an old kitchen. Its cupboards had glass doors so that you could see the dishes in them. There was a musty yet pleasant smell of rich, old wood. The house had a mixture of very old and some newer pieces of furniture. Downstairs was rather dim with all the dark wood and lighting that wasn't fully updated in all the areas. The top floor was the most interesting to me. There was an L-shaped hallway. An old bathtub with claw feet was in the bathroom on one side of the hall. Opposite it was a door to a toilet and small sink. There was a second smaller kitchen on the top floor as well. The dream ended with me walking out the screened front door onto a large wooden porch. I was disappointed to have to leave this warm friendly house.

I woke up with that warm and wonderful sensation which makes it hard to get out of bed.

Comment: I have often dreamed of houses. In my early years, there were nightmares where I was being chased and I would try to find a way out of the house, running down corridors—opening doors that just led to more and more rooms. Even the windows just led to more rooms, kind of like the Winchester Mystery House in San Jose, California. This dream was one of the first that was not a nightmare, and I think that's why it so imprinted in my mind.

This dream stuck with me for a long time because it was simply the kind of house I would love to live in. But, then came another twist. A few months later, I was traveling to Long Island to drop off a friend at college. We decided to stop and see a classmate who had moved with her family to Morrisville, New Jersey along the way. You can probably imagine the shock on my face when we walked up the stairs to the front porch and I said, "I think I've been here before". The house was exactly what I had dreamed. I was so surprised to see a house that really had so much marvelous wood and a bathroom just as I dreamed. Our friend was given the entire top floor as her apartment, while she would be attending a local university. We stayed overnight and left the next day. To this day, I smile when I remember the welcoming warmth of that house.

But what does it mean? Why would God show me this

ahead of time? I'm not really sure, but I do believe the earthy wood and tones along with the short stay remind me that our lives here are temporary. God blesses our lives with many good things, yet we cannot allow ourselves to become too comfortable. The dream of this warm, wonderful house after all the nightmares really did bless me. God used a real house to show me that His deliverance, healing and blessing was just as real as the house I was able to touch, and even sleep in. God really cares about our feelings and our emotional state. He is patient, gentle, loving, kind, and comforting when it comes to healing our broken, bruised, and tormented inner selves.

College Dorm

October 1973: spiritual warfare

I was having one of those dreams where you dream that you woke up. I looked around the room and felt a very evil atmosphere. It was very dark, and I couldn't see anything. I wondered why I would have a bad dream that would leave me feeling like this since God had delivered me from them. I peered through the darkness toward my roommate, asleep in her bed. I could hear her breathing. When I tried to sit up, I realized I was paralyzed. I felt that it was somehow the evil presence in the room holding me down and that I needed to escape. I used all of my strength to roll out of bed. I successfully crashed to the floor and my limbs were each like one hundred pound weights as I crawled toward the door. My roommate did not move or notice the noise from the things that I had knocked off the table as I fell. I guessed the evil presence probably would prevent her from moving as well, so I went to get a neighbor in the room next door to help her.

I pulled myself to my feet using the door handle, which miraculously turned, opening the door. The hallway was brightly lit, and I welcomed the light. I took only one step toward the neighbor's door when she came out hastily in her nightgown. She had heard the crash when I fell, and it registered to her that there was a problem, so she came running. She stopped right in front of me and was about to speak when she "melted." I watched her face and all of the rest of her turn to liquid, just as I was about to touch her arm. I drew back quickly in shock, thinking *she was not really who I thought she was*! My sudden movement woke me up.

I looked around the room, and my roommate was sleeping peacefully. There was no longer any evil presence in the room. I felt an angel had protected me from whatever the enemy had tried to do.

Comment: Again, this is a dream from when I was a very new Christian and new to spiritual warfare. I dreamed I was awake when I wasn't. It was reminiscent of my nightmares, but it wasn't the same because I didn't wake up terrified. In fact, I woke up knowing God had intervened somehow. This was also the last dream of this kind I would ever have—in that I couldn't seem to move, or I thought I was awake when I was not.

This dream assured me once again that God is the God of my sleeping and my waking hours. He watches over us when we are unconscious, so that we can truly rest and have sweet sleep. I believe the enemy had tried one last time to get to my mind, but he was only able to project a few thoughts and nothing more. Even my ability to move in my dream, though with difficulty, was a huge victory compared to previous dreams. God brought complete victory that night in spite of the surroundings.

I was attending my freshman year at a college in Buffalo, New York, where I had experienced some strange encounters with people. I was a new believer and discernment of spirits was not anything I had even heard of before. But I had this sense that there were people there whom I recognized as belonging to the devil—I didn't know what else to call them back them. I could see it in their eyes and could sense the presence of evil at times. I was not walking in righteousness then, either. In fact, probably no one could tell from my actions and attitude that I was a Christian. I did some terrible things that I am not proud of, but they are now covered with the Blood of Jesus and I am forgiven for those days when I walked in such ignorance.

I did tell my roommate and our neighbor, and some others, about the dream and how God had prevented me from harm. This opened the door a bit for me to talk about my faith. As I said, I wasn't a very good Christian example, but they knew my faith in God was real, and it was powerful. (I only attended that college one semester, so I never had contact with any of those people again.)

Baby Crystal

February 1975: prophetic

I dreamed that I had a baby girl. I was holding her and showing her to relatives and several people I didn't know. They were remarking on how cute she was all dressed up in a little white outfit. Someone asked me her name. I answered, "Crystal—like the glass."

Comment: I was seven months pregnant at the time. They didn't do routine ultra-sounds back then so you had to rely upon "old wives tales" to guess the gender of your child. So, I didn't have a clue as to my baby's sex. When I woke up, I knew this wasn't just another dream. I simply understood that it really was from God and that Crystal would be my daughter's name. I had never heard the name before, though years later I found it to be quite popular. A month after the dream I went into labor three weeks early. Our daughter was born, and my husband, although he was not a Christian, did not object to calling her by the name that I had claimed God gave her in my dream.

This was really special to me. I had become pregnant by accident, and the father decided we had to marry, so we did. To my shame, I even had actually considered aborting her. I was married December 20. My husband wrecked our car while driving drunk on December 24, and lost his job two weeks later. At that time, we had gone on welfare, just in time to get Medicaid to cover the birth. I had also had several horrible dreams that my stomach had stretched until it burst open without harming the baby. My skin doesn't stretch properly, and I suffered with extensive stretch marks during my pregnancy. God speaking to me particularly at this time meant that He didn't hate me. I had asked His forgiveness, so this was a major confirmation to me of His acceptance and love for me and our baby.

Jesus Loves Me, This I Know

July 1975: spiritual warfare

I was dreaming an all too familiar dream. Chasing me was a hideous demonic creature. I was running with all my might, but he continued to get closer and closer. We ran up stairs and down, through buildings and across yards. I could hear his cruel taunts. Each sound made my flesh crawl and terror run down my spine. He would kill me, if he could catch me.

I was aware that I had dreamed similar things before. At the last minute, I would wake up in a puddle of sweat and tears. I would lie in my bed feeling alone and terrified though sometimes my husband would still be sleeping beside me. The vision would continue in my head for a long time until exhaustion overcame me, and I fell asleep again. This time, though, it was worse. This demon was very close—I could feel his hot, rancid breath. I thought I would die any moment.

Suddenly I felt, or heard, a tiny sense of God's presence in front of me. I looked up briefly to hear him suggest I sing a song. *A song! I'm about to die! I can't think of a song!* I thought loudly in my mind. I ran a bit more, expecting the talons to tear into my back.

"Sing a song," His firm but gentle voice said.

"Okay, but I can't even think of a scripture. I can't remember a single song!" Again, I strained to look toward the tiny hint of God's Presence, and as I did, the first words came into my head.

"Jesus loves me..." I mouthed and then paused. "This I know..." I was panting the words, with no melody, but I couldn't remember what came next. Then, somehow, just saying those words gave me renewed energy. I looked toward Him again. "For the Bible... The Bible." I paused again to take a short breath. "Tells me so." *YES! I'm remembering!* "Little ones... to Him belong, they are weak... But *He is strong!*"

I looked directly and intently to the now growing Presence of God before me. It was like Light shining in the darkness. As I did, all the words of the song flooded my mind along with a sense that they were as true as the Bible itself and that God was here right now with me. Immediately, there was a shriek from behind me. The demon realized a bit too late that the Presence of God was with me, and he was apparently in terrified pain as he flew in the opposite direction.

Comment: This time as I awoke, I was not in fear at all. I was exhausted but had an overwhelming sense of peace. I immediately fell back to sleep and slept well.

In the days and weeks that followed, I understood better and better that it was when my eyes were turned toward

God that the enemy lost his power over me. God's love overcomes any fear. As time went on, I also learned that as we worship God, He inhabits the praises of His people. Our worship brings Him nearer to us and us to Him. Worship is not just singing songs, but any vehicle with which we express our deepest adoration.

I came to trust God to be with me in any battle and any circumstance that life could throw at me. The more I read His Word, the more I trusted Him. I realized that the book of Psalms are really songs, and in receiving them deep into my heart I gained more confidence in God's Faithfulness and had less fear in my life. I was never again chased like that. I have since then encountered demons in dreams, but under very different conditions, and I have witnessed their fear of God and their demise when they did not submit to His Authority.

> And they overcame him by the blood of the Lamb, and by the word of their testimony; and they loved not their lives unto the death.
>
> Revelation 12:11

Car Door Smashed

August 1975: prophetic

I dreamed that our car was spinning and sliding. I wasn't in it, and I knew that our daughter wasn't in it. It came to rest in the middle of a yard—I couldn't tell which way the road even was. The back door on the passenger side had a hole in the middle of it, as if someone had punched it in with a giant spike.

Comment: I woke up to the doorbell ringing. I ran downstairs quickly so that it wouldn't wake up my infant daughter. A police officer was standing there with some papers. He asked my name and if I owned a 1978 Oldsmobile, Delta 88. "Yes."

Did I know it was left on the lawn at 5298 Jennings Road?

"No, my husband went to work yesterday and has not returned home," I said as I looked in the driveway, half hoping to see the car. The officer was actually quite nice and finally agreed for me to make arrangements to move the car rather than paying for towing and to speak with the owners about repairing the damage in their yard.

I made some phone calls, and soon all was resolved. My husband had been, once again, drunk with a friend. The car spun-out, and they walked to his friend's house. God bless those people for being so understanding. When the car finally came home, I went out to see if I needed to wash caked mud from it. I was shocked when I saw the big hole in the side of the back passenger door. I had forgotten about the dream, until I saw it. I was able to determine later that they had earlier hit a guardrail. Thank God, no one was hurt.

This was representative of the early days of my marriage for fourteen years to a good, kind man—who struggled with alcoholism. This is the life some wives live. I was a new Christian, and God used these things to assure me I was not alone. God was watching every detail of our lives, and I could trust Him even if I couldn't trust anyone else. He is forever faithful. I thank God for these reassurances back then; they kept me on track and hopeful in God, rather than giving up or giving in to sin in my own life.

A Hurricane & a Palm Tree

June 1978: prophetic

We were in an apartment building along a beach at evening. There were a few people in the apartment. I assumed they were my friends or neighbors, but I don't know who they were. They were joking about having lived through hurricanes and bad storms. I turned and looked out at the ocean. The wind was blowing strongly. It was raining hard, and the sea and sky looked ominous as night approached. These people were unafraid, even as the storm grew worse. The rain began to hit the window to the balcony so hard you could see nothing through the glass.

    Suddenly, there was a crash as the entire place collapsed under the weight of an apparent tidal wave. I immediately realized I was being ejected into the wave of water many feet deep. I couldn't tell which way was up or down. I knew instinctively to hold my breath as long as I could. The other thing I knew I must do was hold on to the baby now under my arm. Even if it drowned, there would be a chance to revive it once I got to the surface. I opened my eyes to a torrent of water, bubbles and debris. I had to try to determine which way was up toward the precious air my lungs were screaming for and for the sake of this baby.

I suddenly saw a huge palm tree floating past me. *Eventually it will pop up on top of the water and float*, I thought, so I grabbed hold of it with all the strength in my free arm. I wondered if I would hurt the baby, as I was trying so hard to hold on. The water seemed to be pulling me in one direction and the baby and palm tree in other directions though somehow, with God's help, I hung on. Suddenly, it burst through the surface like a torpedo, with me holding on for life. We were soon washed up onto land.

Comment: Although I did live in Florida for a few months once, I never experienced any storms of this sort. I am not one to stick around to see what might happen. Instead, I always opt for safety. So, it was strange for me to find myself in such a situation. The other really strange thing was that I was holding a baby. My daughter was about three years old when I had this dream, and I did not plan to have any more children, ever. So whose baby could this have been?

It is amazing to me that I had the sense of thinking objectively and totally without panic through this entire ordeal. I had the sense that my survival depended on my remaining level headed and doing the right thing. Quick decisions were essential. I mostly had the sense that if I did what was correct, God would provide a way of escape. Though I thought it might be impossible, He did just that.

It wasn't until years later that I came to understand more of this dream. The people were ignoring the obvious danger and even mocking the idea that they could even *be* in danger. The baby would have represented something in my life that I held precious—something from God. It could be a ministry or an ideal or principle, something that I knew God didn't want me to let go of—even if it meant I would drown myself trying to preserve it. I think, at the time I had this dream, it was my salvation and understanding of God as my Lord and Savior. My own immature Christianity was the baby. You see I was saved only a few years, but I had never been to a church, never been baptized. I didn't know any other real believers. My teaching was from the Word of God, by reading the Bible, and listening to an occasional Christian radio program. A year later, I found a church, and I have been rooted in good teaching since that time.

The wave and the floodwaters represent being swept away. It could be the world and its devastating circumstance that could come crashing down on us. The pull of the world can almost drown us. Certainly it can confuse us so we no longer see clearly which way is up. It could also have been God's judgment on the world and their disregard of God. The floodwaters could have been sweeping me away from the grip of this world.

It is also very interesting that it was a palm tree. A palm tree speaks to me of God's grace and mercy. Prophetically a palm tree can indicate triumph over death or victory. I didn't really know to hold on to that, it just happened to be the thing God sent to rescue me. Isn't He *amazing*?!

Car Crash

July 1978: prophetic, provision

I was riding in the back seat of a copper colored sedan, with a black interior. My sister-in-law was in the front passenger seat, and her boyfriend was driving. They were having a conversation. I was very upset because he was driving too fast. I don't trust other drivers in general—I usually prefer do the driving myself. I was talking to her, asking why he was being so careless. He was simply ignoring me. Then he lost control of the car! The next thing I knew the car was careening down a very steep slope. There were lots of young trees and saplings that the car hit as it hurled downward. Striking the rocks and trees caused the car to jerk and bang uncontrollably from side to side.

It's funny how your mind thinks in crisis situations. I perceived the driver was probably dead and that his foot was pressing the gas pedal, even as gravity was pulling us continually downward. By this time, the interior of the car was smashed, and I was pinned under the back of the front seat, unable to see or move. The seat was coming down heavily on my back. As the front of the car continued to crush, the seat also was crushing me as it moved toward the backseat.

I could feel my rib cage and back, cracking and breaking. There was nothing I could do but listen to the thud of another impact and feel the increasing pressure. I suddenly realized that I wasn't really in any pain. It was as if a flood of heat was filling my torso—I reasoned that this was what it must feel like to bleed internally. I was puzzled by the lack of pain. I couldn't feel my legs at all. Feeling myself black out, I woke up.

Comment: I was still quite new to these types of dreams that weren't nightmares. It seemed to me, I probably died, but there was no fear—and *no* pain! I woke up thankful to God that He protected me from the pain and fear. And I vowed *never* to ride with that driver again in my life! I wondered if the car and its color were significant—no one I knew had a car like this.

When I was young, probably around eight, I remember wondering what it would be like when I die. I had never thought about it before. I even remember standing in the upstairs bathroom just staring at the floor thinking. Somehow, I decided that there would be pain and then darkness. Hopefully, it would be like sleeping, because being underground with bugs and worms crawling on me was more than I could take—if I had any consciousness. I never let myself think about it again. This dream, gave me reassurance that God would be with me, even in death. Was it possible that I would be in a situation where I was so out of control that my life would be in danger like this? I suppose, it could. However, I knew that, if it did, God would be in it and take care of me never the less.

Now I understand that God was saving me from the danger I was in, but then, I was just learning to trust Him *through* the danger itself—not only to save me from it. The car and its driver represented the natural world that felt very much out of my control at the time. Bronze prophetically can mean a demoted or impoverished state. The black interior represented the darkness of sin. Man's natural wisdom and abilities are in opposition to the wisdom of God. Even as a young Christian, my friends would only tolerate listening to just so much of *my* kind of wisdom, which I claimed was what the Bible said. I was living my life in such a vehicle—impoverished, still uncovering past layers of sin, and generally feeling out of control—on a collision course. Sometimes it can take breaking our backs to get our lives aligned with the will and purposes of God. I have survived only by the grace of God.

Grocery Store Shooting

March 1979: spiritual warfare

I was walking up and down the aisle of a grocery store in a hurry to get a few items. Suddenly, I heard shots and simultaneous screams. It sounded like an automatic weapon, just a couple aisles from where I was standing.

Terrified, I peered into the next aisle to see if people were all right. I saw women huddled on the floor next to their shopping carts, crying. They looked unhurt, but as I watched, a man in dark clothes walked to the head of the aisle saw the women and shot them repeatedly. My heart was in my throat. I kept still, afraid to make any telltale sound. I could hear another man with a gun walking in the other direction. Apparently, they were going aisle to aisle, killing everyone in the store. I crawled close to these women and rolled in the puddle of blood, hoping it would look as though I was also shot. I lay on my side, hoping my breathing would not give me away.

I heard crying and screaming as the men methodically

went through the store. Then all was quiet. They walked back toward the center of the store to the aisle where I was laying. But they weren't quite satisfied. They decided to shoot more rounds into the dead bodies before they left. Mine was one of the last ones they shot at. I felt the bullets like heat, enter into my back the five or six times. I was shot. There was no pain, just heat. My eyes opened as I stared at the poor dead women on the floor in front of me, expecting to join them, and then I woke up.

Comment: As I woke up I could still feel the heat in my back for a few seconds. I thought, *Why did I have such a dream?* I had victory over nightmares, but this was a dream about men—not demons. Obviously, they were evil, bad men—but still men. And unlike many of my dreams, I was unable to help anyone, not even myself. But the thing I remembered most was that I did *not* pray in this dream. I understood that demons had to obey the Name of Jesus and could not trespass past the Blood. However, man doesn't always understand such boundaries. The innocent blood all around on the floor was evidence to me.

I also learned that although I said I trusted God, I reverted to coming up with an idea that represents man's wisdom to protect myself in this situation. I put man's blood on me to disguise myself as dead. It is the Blood of Jesus that we need to cover us to cleanse, redeem, and protect us. We are to die to our flesh, not try to preserve it. Our life is in Jesus.

I have since then learned that God intervenes in the affairs of man as we pray and give Him the authority to do so. The men may not have obeyed if I said, "Stop in the Name of Jesus." Although I now know that they might have stopped, if they were demonically controlled. But we are to pray and ask for God's protection and God's intervention—as the scriptures clearly state. Sometimes the simple prayer, "Jesus!" is all that is needed. God can send an angel to deflect a bullet or a blow. He can cause the enemy (in this case mere men) to see hosts of police officers or angels coming so that they run away. God can and will intervene. I learned a valuable lesson about always trusting and depending on God. Even if it means calling those things that are not as if they were, if necessary. Praise God!

Jesus' Office

November 1980: vision of God

I was on an elevator going up. It was not like any elevator I had ever seen, or even heard of. It was spacious, very well lit and the walls appeared to be made of metal, but the metal was neither silver, nor gold, nor brass colored; it was kind of all the colors of metal mixed together as one. It was beautiful as if the metal was itself a gem. As I gazed at this amazing looking metal, I realized it was both solid and transparent as well. If I looked at it just right, I could see cables outside that were pulling the elevator up. I glanced behind me. Where I had previously looked and seen only a solid metal wall, I could faintly see through the wall to an amazing view of the world beyond. We were *very* high up!

I had only a moment to look, when the door opened on the side that had the cables. I stepped out into a corridor of the most prestigious office building I could ever have imagined. I felt like taking only one slow step at a time so that I could take in all of these magnificent surroundings. Something, however, kept pushing me forward. There was a door to my left, which was open. I stepped inside, knowing this was where my appointment was, though I had no idea what the appointment was for.

There was a huge, expansive mahogany desk with someone sitting in its chair, facing the opposite wall. The chair slowly spun around to face me, and I suddenly knew whose office this was. Jesus Himself stood up to greet me. I looked down at the floor; I could not look into His face. He motioned for me to look to His right at the wall. There was a giant whiteboard covered with words. More than that, they were grouped in paragraphs. My attention went to a scrolling screen in the bottom right hand corner. There were dates and words scrolling by. I could almost read the dates... at least the years... as the dates went by with accompanying descriptions of just one or two words. It seemed as the dates scrolled off the screen, any sins, mistakes or bad memories of those dates were scrolling out of my memory to be gone forever.

The screen slowed and then stopped on a date. It was yesterday, November 21. Before I could try to read the words, He spoke to me. I looked down at my feet once again, as He asked me, "Do these dates mean anything to you?" My heart and tongue faltered. All that came out of my mouth was, "I..." My mind was flooded with the past three days of preparation for the holidays. I had wanted to bless my in-law family, and make the most memorable Thanksgiving dinner for them. I used new recipes and wanted to show them God's love by breaking my back through preparation for this very special meal—cornbread-chestnut stuffing, pumpkin soup served in a real pumpkin, dinner rolls from made from scratch, homemade cranberry sauce, and several special pies—the works. But even with all my great intentions, I had not taken time to even glance at my Bible, nor offer a moment's praise or prayer to God during the entire two days prior to Thanksgiving.

At this time, I considered God the most important person in my life. The thought that I had neglected Him for three days was almost too much for me to bear. I loved Him so much, and I could sense His pain and loss of my fellowship. My heart felt as though it was broken beyond repair at disappointing Him. I stood speechless, motionless, my eyes tightly shut—not knowing what to do or say. I was *so* guilty.

The next thing I knew, He had come around the side of the desk and was standing next to me. Placing His arm lovingly around me, He made me know, with only a touch, that all the dates with mistakes had been removed from His memory as well. He had only memories of my love and my fellowship with Him. Suddenly, I understood that even as I was sorry in my heart and repentant before Him who had already paid for every time I might fall short, I was forgiven. I was loved.

He spoke to me in a gentle voice, barely whispering in my ear and said, "There are many good and wonderful things in my memory of our relationship; there is only one thing you lack… I created you as you are physically." I suddenly understood that the Lord thought I was beautiful, just as He created me. I often held my own body in contempt. I was struck as with a blow to my chest that knocked me right out of heaven and heavily planted me back on the earth, as I awoke.

Comment: The blow was not physical, yet my heart remained heavy for a very long time as though it was. I had grown up with such a low self-esteem that it had affected every aspect of my life. I was a perfectionist who flopped between being an overachiever and wallowing in self-pity, unable to do anything. My hatred of self was centered on my own physical body. I looked in the mirror and saw a disaster. Any parts of me that might not be considered totally bad appeared strangely out of place, like they belonged on someone else's body. It was a strange view, not unlike those with anorexia, who gaze into the mirror and see a very distorted view—not reality.

But God is so gracious. His love was the part of the dream that overshadowed my choice to spend time with Him those next few days. His love penetrated the self-hatred I had. God had hugged me! God had created me exactly as I am! He loves me as I am, and His forgiveness goes into the past and the future. This was a whole new reality for me to adjust to.

Other things I noted from this dream were that back in 1980, there was no such thing as a white board, yet today that is definitely what I would call it—I saw this same kind of board in another dream in 1986 though with no scrolling window. The scrolling window looked a lot like a computer monitor, which I did see some twelve years later. Although flat screens like this one described here are much newer. It seems the Lord communicates in ways that we can relate to even if we don't yet know what things are, years later we can see even more clearly how God is speaking to us in ways that intentionally transcend the years. His Word is always current. This has helped my mind to better comprehend the difficulties the prophets have had in writing what they would see. As I read books like Ezekiel or Revelation, I have an expanded view of the possibilities contained in their limited ability to express what they saw.

God was not only teaching me to bring me gently to the next level in Him, but was also preparing me to receive much, much more down the road. God is so multifaceted and multilayered, as the Bible says in Romans 11:33, "O the depth of the riches both of the wisdom and knowledge of God! How unsearchable are his judgments, and his ways past finding out!" But He keeps reaching out to us saying, "Call unto me, and I will answer you, and show you great and mighty things, which you knew not" (Jeremiah 33:3).

He is the Lord of Hosts

WAREHOUSE RUINS & A ROUND CHURCH

September 1981: end times, spiritual warfare

I was hiding. I was close beside a cement block wall trying to blend in with the rubble around me. I could tell by the size of the perimeter that the building had been of good size. Like a warehouse, where they would have stored food or goods of some sort. But the tin roof looked as if it had caved in some time ago. It was pushed aside toward one corner of the area, partially crumpled. Someone had attempted to clean up the area as to leave nowhere to hide.

Someone began shooting in my direction, but apparently, they couldn't see me. The shots were hitting randomly in areas of the ruins. As the shooting stopped, I peered between the broken places in the remains of the wall. I could see no one, nothing, yet I had the sense I needed to lay low or I would be seen. I waited, until it felt as though I were alone, or at least my heart had started to pound less. All the while, I prayed that God would show me how to get away.

I took off quickly through the rear of the structure and

across a field. I kept low to the ground as I half ran, ready to dive into the tall grass if I saw or heard anything. I didn't know where I was headed though. I quickly crossed a road and lay down in the ditch beside it. In front of me was a round building. There was a front door and a back door. A broken sign near the front door told me it was a church. I went to the front door to see if anyone was inside, I expected it would be a possible refuge, if the enemy hadn't gotten there first. Arriving at the door, I was joined by another person arriving discreetly from the opposite direction. I indicated to them not to rush in, as the enemy was everywhere by this time.

We entered the room, which had been ransacked and ruined. There was a man that entered the room from a side room and I could do nothing except shout at him, "In the Name of Jesus get out!" As he left through the back door, I knew there would be others just outside the back door waiting for us. I felt as if we had walked into a trap, but the power of the Name of Jesus had worked. Perhaps if we stayed there we could use it to keep them away from us—but for how long?

Comment: I was still very new to spiritual warfare when I had this dream. It was revelation to me that men would react to the Name of Jesus as I had seen demons do. This dream showed me how God could seemingly make me invisible. Those shooting could shoot to every corner of the place. There wasn't a place to hide effectively—so they should have seen me. God also showed me how I could be attuned to the Spirit and know when to move or stay still. I had a real sense of being guided when I desperately needed to be. I also was surprised that I was the one to caution the other person since I normally took a passive role. The church offered only temporary safety; danger was at the door. Though we had refuge in the church building, the refuge was really only in the Name of Jesus, just as the scriptures say over and over in the Psalms, He is our high tower and our refuge.

This was one of the early dreams when I began to understand that everything in my life was about training. We will one day need to know God's voice and trust Him to miraculously guide us in order to save us from very evil times and people. But, we are never to fear what man may do to us, to live is Christ, to die is gain (Hebrews 13:6 and Philippians 1:21). May my life glorify God—each and every moment.

The Car that would not Start

January 1982: provision, prophetic

I was running up and down bare hillsides. The grass wasn't very tall, but it was high enough to make it difficult to run. There was a dirt roadway, but I had the feeling that I would be caught quicker if I used that path. Someone was chasing me. I was aware that I was dreaming, and I was wondering why I was having this sort of dream. I had gotten victory over nightmares. Somehow, this was different. Those chasing me weren't the previous demonic types, hideous, and scary looking. These were more like men, perhaps men that hated Christians. I sensed they really wanted to catch me, and it was almost my *duty* to get away.

As I came to the top of a hill there was a car parked. It was an older car. It looked as though it might have been abandoned. I ran to it, not wanting to waste any time if it wasn't going to be my form of escape. As I approached the rusty vehicle from the driver's side, I could see the keys in the ignition. I decided to give it a shot. I jumped into the driver's seat and tried to start the car. Nothing. Not even a click that the solenoid makes. Nothing. I breathed out, "Lord, if you want me to do this..."

I could hear the men in the distance. I had wasted precious time and now there was no turning back. Then a voice inside of me said, "Start the car and *drive*!"

I'm arguing in my head, *I already tried this*. But I closed the door and obeyed. I turned the key in the ignition. No sound but in obedience and pure faith, I put the car into drive. My first reaction was amazement. The car actually went into drive. There was absolutely no sound, no vibration, to indicate the engine was running. This bolstered my faith so that as the men came over the top of the hill I stepped hard on the gas pedal expecting the car to move.

Even though I expected it, I was shocked as the car leaped forward. I took off leaving a cloud of dust that obstructed the men from view. I had escaped. Praise God!

Comment: This dream was strange to me in several ways; that's why I remember it so well. I was aware that I was dreaming, yet I went ahead and participated in the dream. I had the sense that God was directing me the entire time. I am not sure if the enemy was preventing me from sensing that the car had started, or if my faith somehow activated angelic assistance that made it as if the car were running, but it was a great lesson to me that if we obey God we can expect the miraculous—miraculous provision and miraculous protection. I didn't have time to pray about it and get a confirmation. I had to choose instantly to trust and obey

God with my very life. As I have continued to remember this dream over the years, it has been a strong reminder that God does indeed direct our steps, in every detail and He honors our faith.

Woman in a Coma

March 1982: spiritual warfare

I saw a room with a hospital bed and rather stark surroundings—a straight-backed chair, a bedside table, a window. The room appeared empty, except for a small figure in the bed under the covers. In this dream, it wasn't as if I was there walking around the room, more like looking at a picture or video monitor except I could see in every direction to every corner of the room.

I looked closer at the tiny, frail figure lost in the bed. It was a small, very thin woman with dark hair curled up like a child. As I looked, I became aware of a woman sitting in the straight-backed chair across the room. The chair had appeared empty a moment before.

Instantly, I saw that this woman had the same hair and features, though not quite as gaunt looking. She was sitting up straight, with a look of distress on her face. A demonic creature sat on her shoulders, its talons dug deeply into her so that she was unable to move even her head. The creature, looking like a hideous bat with folded up wings and disgusting leathery skin, perched heavily on top of her. She was forced to face directly at her own figure in the bed.

Nurses and others came and went from the room, checking on the figure in the bed, adjusting tubes, etc. They paid no attention to the woman in the chair; she was as invisible as I was. I could hear them chat about the weather and make comments about the status of the woman in the bed. As they talked, I could see in the woman's eyes that she saw and heard all that happened in that room—with a tortured inability to respond.

Comment: I woke up the next morning and went about my housewife duties as usual, not even remembering the dream. Then I heard on the radio the mention of Karen Quinlan, who had been in a coma for years. Immediately, my dream flooded back and I realized the dream was about her. Karen had been declared completely brain dead. When they disconnected her from the machines that were keeping her alive, she was supposed to die quickly. But she did not; she lived for another nine years. This was a very publicized event in our nation's history. I didn't have access to newspapers or TV at the time, so I was mostly unaware until that day.

Over the next few months, I did some research, finding information in newspapers and such. (We didn't have the Internet back then, and I had two toddlers in diapers.) I prayed for her. I prayed for her salvation, not knowing or understanding if it were possible for a body so close to death to recover even with God's miracles. In my research, I found that her father would faithfully come and read the Bible to her, almost every day. When I heard this, I dug up an address and wrote him a letter to encourage him that God had showed me she could see and hear and urged him to continue blessing his daughter in this way. She died in 1985. I personally feel we will see her in heaven. Even her father, a Catholic, could not have understood how the Word of God brought life to a soul literally on the edge of eternity. I believe that the day she chose to embrace the Word from God and His grace—demonstrated in receiving Salvation through Jesus, that demon had to release her. And at that moment, the Lord took her into His everlasting arms of comfort.

That is what I understood the Lord was showing me in this dream. I joined my faith with her father's, for Karen's salvation. Most importantly, my faith and prayers have changed toward all who might be considered hopeless, whether they are ill or well. God loves us so much that He will not allow us to suffer one moment more than necessary for our good.

Preacher in Pink

July 1982: heaven

I was in an auditorium filled with people. It was huge. So huge, I could not distinguish individuals as far back as it went in every direction. It was much like those massive open-air gatherings in Africa led by Reinhardt Bohnke with multitudes of people. I was sitting in the center, near the front, about twenty rows back. I was looking around at the strange variety of people—old, young, rich, poor, cultured and well, let's say some scummy looking hicks. What could this place be?

Then, something was happening on the platform in front of us. There was worship music coming from everywhere, as the place seemed to come into one voice, one sound. But the music wasn't from a "worship team" at least not one you could see. It was as if they filled the room—I assumed it must be angels, and we just couldn't see them. Movement on the platform again caught my attention. A man was preparing to speak.

The music subsided, and the man began speaking. He was really giving a testimony of how he was supposed to have been a preacher, but he didn't believe what he said himself. Yet God had mercy on him, and brought him to a low place where he saw himself as he really was. Then he went on and on, thanking God for His mercy and grace. The strange thing about him was that he was dressed in a pink, sparkly suit and white shiny shoes. It was hard for me to listen to him because his clothes were so distracting. How could anyone have taken him seriously when he had pretended to be a preacher on earth?

On earth! It suddenly hit me that I was witnessing his testimony on the other side, in Heaven! Again, I looked around me at the throngs of diverse people. Now it made sense. Was there anyone I knew? I then realized that sitting right beside me was my mother and father. They were two people I did not expect to see there at all. My father, who had been totally disillusioned by the church when I was just a child, was listening intently and really into what the man in the pink suit had to say. That was certainly *not* my father, as I knew him! He wouldn't listen to any preacher, let alone one in a pink suit! We soon left that place because they wanted to take me somewhere else to see something or someone.

The next thing I remember is walking up a pathway with the most beautiful green grass on either side of it. I was really noticing how green and absolutely beautiful the grass was. When I looked up, there a few feet ahead of us I saw my grandmother, my mother's mother. I remembered her as the meanest woman I had ever met. I was afraid of her all my life. She was the opposite of all the things that you read about warm, loving, doting grandmothers. In total shock, I stopped. Then I remembered that my mother had said that they discovered her dead in her bed with her Bible open to Psalm 23. She was smiling. It looked strange because I didn't recall ever seeing her smile. I don't know how I even recognized her; she looked so different.

Comment: My parents are still living. My grandmother had passed away about ten years before I had this dream. I am so thankful for God's forgiveness. The woman I had known, the results of many difficult years that had hardened her, had passed away—but the real person inside of her, who must have loved the Lord, was still living. I know if my dream had continued that she would have welcomed me into heaven with those big arms smothering me in all the love that had been withheld for so many years.

My parents too have softened in these twenty years since I had this dream. I found that my mother knew the Lord when she was a teenager. She had even taught Sunday school for a short time before her parents forbade her from attending church. She had not returned even after marriage. When I had this dream, I was not convinced of their belief in Jesus in any significant way. A few years after this dream, the Lord healed her of lung cancer—while she was on the operating table. The doctors were amazed. The tumor suddenly disappeared, thanks to the prayers of my young children who had the faith to believe. At that time my mother began attending church and has slowly grown in her faith and become more tolerant of my more extreme way of living my Christian faith. My father does not attend services but is not opposed to her attending. One day he will understand how much God loves him and receive his salvation.

The Lord taught me a life long lesson about judging others through this dream. We don't know what motivates people; we don't know where their hearts are with God. We *must* ask God how to love them, how even to pray for them, so that we don't condemn them with our words. God does not ignore sin, He brings us to the place where we repent of it and turn away from our sin. When we turn away from sin to embrace Him, He covers our past with the Blood of Jesus, and He remembers the sin no more. May we all see ourselves and others through God's eyes—*always*.

Plane Crash on a Bridge

September 1982: airplane

I was in an airplane flying over a large city. I assumed it was New York City, as that is the biggest city near where I lived at the time. The plane was a smaller jet, about the size of a Boeing 717 today. The plane was in trouble. We were losing altitude very quickly. Some buildings were looming taller than we were. The people in the plane seemed to be in shock. There was no sound, maybe whimpering, but they all just stared, bracing for an impact.

Then my vision was from outside the plane. I could see this plane and its pilots desperately searching for the safest place to put the plane down. The river ahead looked much less dangerous than the mass of buildings below. As they banked it toward the river, the aircraft did not respond as it should. The plane only half turned and headed directly toward an arched bridge. The pilot painstakingly attempted to guide the plane through the arches parallel to and just above where the cars were driving. Of course, the bridge wasn't quite a wide as the wingspan of the plane, so first the tip of the right wing was torn off, then the tip of the left as we bumped our way through crashing into the lanes of highway just beyond the bridge. We then skidded to a stop. I couldn't believe I was still alive though some of the people were obviously dead. I woke up in shock, yet understanding that a miracle had happened.

Comment: As I have said, I once had nightmares. Many of these were short stints of walking in my deepest fears. I had a lot of fear as a child. I had abnormal fears of things like airplanes, elevators, and earthquakes, even things like bees, snakes, and rats. I was tormented at night by my own imagination and demonic influences. When God healed me and gave me victory over those fears in my dreams, He also gradually gave me the ability to face all my fears in daily life and live victoriously body, mind, and spirit. This dream reflects the beginning of my victory over the fear of flying. I still wouldn't fly in an airplane after this for a while, but it was a step in the direction of learning to trust God.

The airplane and the bridge indicate a transitioning between the earthly and heavenly realms. The plane, while crashing, went over a bridge that land vehicles would normally use. There were casualties, but I survived. This is a cruel, evil, difficult world. The god of this world, Satan, would destroy us all, yet the Lord uses even the man-made things of this world to accomplish His purposes. Even when the situation appears impossible, God is in control. He always causes us to triumph in Christ. This dream was one of those steps up the ladder of faith and trust in God as well as understanding the ways and heart of our Lord and Savior.

Peace Which Passes All Understanding

October 1984: vision of God

> This wasn't a dream. I was fully conscious when I saw Jesus. And yes, I immediately recognized Him.

We had planned to have our fourth child at home. I had spoken to the mid-wife on the phone just a week before, making plans to call her when I first went into labor, knowing she would get there when she could. We were not concerned as we had been through the routine three times previously with no difficulties. The placenta delivery would kind of take its time but would not be a problem. My labors had not been too difficult, and the babies had come quicker each time. The last baby I had delivered in about three to four hours.

We were living in a small travel trailer. I awoke suddenly at five o'clock in the morning with a sharp pain in my stomach. It was exactly my due date. The pain was excruciating, not like a labor pain that rose in intensity and then lessened. I barely caught my breath and it happened again. My groans woke my husband and we began a fifty-minute intense time of blurred pain and anticipation. At 5:50, our daughter was born, but we were shocked to see that she was quite bluish, and there was no pulse in the umbilical cord. We tried fruitlessly to revive her. Then my husband ran to a payphone to call for an ambulance.

We did not know that my placenta had prematurely separated, causing the baby to receive no oxygen and me to hemorrhage. She was already in the birth canal, so the blood did not come until after she cleared the passageway. I didn't realize the dangerous amount of blood seeping out of me as I held her and waited. My pain had stopped, and I didn't deliver the placenta. I whispered, "Oh, God," in a pleading, helpless, confused, mother's voice.

Suddenly I realized Jesus was sitting at the end of the bed. He was completely relaxed, His hands folded across His lap, palms up. As I rubbed her back, I said to Him, "She didn't even get to feel her mother's touch, her hugs..."

He interrupted me and said, "*She went from the warmth and safety of a mother's womb directly into my arms—what more could a mother want?*" Suddenly I knew that this child would never know anything except warmth, love and loving embraces. She did not even experience the trauma of birth. He would be taking care of her, ever so much better than we ever could. Everything was going to be all right after all. His Peace flooded my soul—it was almost tangible.

I was calm when my husband came in moments later with the ambulance crew. They couldn't get a stretcher through the door so they helped me walk that far, about five feet. I was almost to the door when I passed out the first time. I was in and out of consciousness for the next few hours until I was finally given two pints of blood and the explanation of what had happened to us both. Little did I know that when Jesus visited, He not only gave me His peace but also *my life*.

His peace continued to sustain me over the following weeks. I was discharged from the hospital in two days (due to inability to pay), only to discover we had been evicted. Our car, which hadn't started in weeks, suddenly started and drove us four hours away to an abandoned horse farm where we took refuge. I hadn't been given any medication, so I developed a severe breast infection and was delirious for a week. I had no medication, no food—only water. I don't know how my husband and children survived that week on twenty dollars. My husband wouldn't talk about it, and my children don't remember. (I think they went fishing and cooked on a campfire.) Still God had promised me everything would be all right, and it was. We survived. We all grew stronger and closer as a family—and especially closer to God. We saw many miracles take place during the next months. God healed relationships in my newly saved husband's family, and we were able to go back to our hometown (twelve hours away) five months later. The car continued to run, sometimes only on gas fumes, I think.

THE WHITEBOARD

November 1986: heaven, prophetic

I was sitting in a booth, similar to a restaurant, alone. There were others scattered throughout the room. They appeared to be groups of one or two people, or small families. The booths were a red material; the tables were made of some kind of stone. There were servants, not really like waiters or waitresses. I could tell by their demeanor that they were attempting to administer to the individuals personally, not like a waiter whose job is to serve, but their boss's desires is their real concern. They might be very professional or very personal, but these servants were more like personal ministers. They occasionally brought food, but usually they would usher people to another room.

I watched them bring the man in the next booth something to eat. He immediately began eating. I realized I was staring, as they brought me a bowl of the same thing. I cannot describe what it was. At first glance, it looked like something you might call macaroni and cheese, though it wasn't. It wasn't the same consistency, and though I only got to taste it, it tasted almost sweet in my mouth—but not like dessert sweet. It was good. It was apparently a heavenly-fast-food of sorts, providing something until you arrived where you needed to be.

I only got a taste because two of the "servants" came to my table immediately after the bowl was set before me. They looked at one another, then me, indicating I was to come with them. But we didn't leave the room. I stood and faced the center of the room where there appeared a huge white board. One servant would point to one spot on the board as writing appeared. I hardly had time to read what was written when the other would point to another area. Back and forth, for a very long time, I read and read and read. More and more words would appear then disappear and be replaced with new information. Suddenly, it stopped. Again, the servants looked at one another and then indicated to me that it was time to leave. Leave, and go back to earth.

I thought, *What!*? *How am I supposed to remember so much stuff? This is like memorizing vast encyclopedia collections in mere minutes! How will I remember?* They said, when I needed to know the information, I would remember. They said it both at the same time, together. I knew instantly that it was true. Only God could have given this information to me, and only God can retrieve it.

Comment: As I woke up, I tried in earnest to see one glimpse of the board with my mind's eye, and remember even one thing written there. All I could see was the huge white board. My memory of any words or letters was blocked, but I had the overwhelming sense that an awesome responsibility had been placed on my shoulders. It was more information than I had ever considered that a person could retain. Yet I knew that when God wants me to recall anything, in His time, it will be there. So I have to just let this sit, while I ponder in my heart, *Why? Why, would I need to know this kind of stuff and who would I one day be telling it to? Why didn't God tell them directly?* But, I fully understand that His ways are higher than ours, and past finding out (Isaiah 55:9, Job 9:10, Romans 11:33).

I believe the red seats speak of the Blood of Jesus and stone was used as a reminder of a covenant. The food would probably be a type of provision—as for a journey. The entire scenario speaks to me of God's covenant with man and His promise in the Last Days to intervene in the affairs of men to accomplish His purposes, preserve and protect his bride—while He brings her to a place of perfection and maturity, defeating the enemy in the process. The two angels also speak of covenant. I sensed this was God's yea and amen, a surety that this would come to pass.

Later, when I first came to Israel on a prayer tour in 2002, I had my first flash back of seeing a part of the vision of this white board (sixteen years before). The letters were in black, and were, I am quite certain, in Hebrew. This has happened several times since. Curiously, I am just now beginning to study Biblical Hebrew on a part-time basis. If I was reading that board so quickly back then and I didn't even know the language—yet I retained the information—that is astounding. God is truly awesome!

Firing Squad

February 1989: end times

I was standing with three of my children and many more people on the edge of a deep ditch. We were facing a line of soldiers, and it was very cold; yet no one moved or made a sound. We were all naked. I whispered to my children, without moving my lips, to look across the ditch to something on the other side. Don't look at me, don't look at each other, don't look at the other people standing in the cold with us, and especially don't look at the soldiers. The children, ages two to eight, were so scared they obeyed without a peep.

I prayed again to God. He had answered my earlier prayer to shield the children's eyes, that they would not see the nakedness—not theirs nor the others. God had enabled us to remain together to strengthen one another. Now I prayed that the bullets from the soldier's guns would kill the children instantly, so that they would not suffer and would not even realize what had happened to us all. God had given supernatural grace as we stood in the cold. I could see and feel that the children were protected from the shame and horror of the situation. During my prayer of thanksgiving, shots suddenly rang out. We fell forward in unison onto the heap of rotting corpses in the ditch just below us. We didn't fall far. I could see that again my prayers had been answered. My children had passed to the next life with only peace on their faces. Then I realized it was I who was still alive. I could see and hear yet I was afraid to move, wondering why I was alive and what I would have to face next. I couldn't even tell if I was shot, or bleeding. I couldn't feel anything due to the numbing cold.

Comment: I have since read accounts like this from the Holocaust. Villages in Poland (and other areas) had this happen to them. I am not Polish and I am not Jewish, yet I have felt their pain. When I had this dream, I didn't know about these things. In my mind, I thought it was probably a preview of the last days. My children had already grown past the ages they were in the dream, so I didn't understand that the dream could be the future or a connection with the Jewish people. Nothing in our past would take on this symbolism. It was disturbing, yet there was peace—even during the dream. God's grace was so real; it was almost tangible. I especially remember the feeling of relief, not remorse, as the children died mercifully.

Many years later, I read and became familiar with horrors like this that took place during the Nazi Holocaust, yet I was not strong enough to face the pictures and memories in the Yad VaShem Memorial in Jerusalem until 2003—my fourth opportunity to visit. God's grace has given me that strength and a sense of hope as well, partly because I had this dream and I know how His strength and peace can penetrate anything. I can empathize with the Jewish people as few Gentiles can.

Today I see the dream differently. I see the children as spiritual children or even ministries, and the event as an end time possibility. However, the focus remains on the grace and peace of God to go with us through every valley. Our lives are in His hands. We can trust Him; His grace is sufficient. Some believers will be saved from the clutches of the wicked through early deaths (Isaiah 57:1, 2). Others will stand and be overcomers (Revelation 12:1). All who prevail will share in the victory of the Lord Jesus, the True Messiah (Revelation 21:7).

Among the
Mountain Peaks

June 1989: heaven

I was standing among the peaks of an extremely high mountain range. They were jagged and pointed, but they were green all the way to the top, not rocky and frozen, as I would expect. I was standing there, sort of on air, floating among the peaks. Ahead of me was Heaven, with the typical and wonderful green, grassy expanse looking toward hills and a mountain in the very far distance. But my attention was downward. I heard a voice say to me, "If you look down from here you can see the affairs of men." I don't know what my real concern was, or what I thought I was looking for. But I began scanning the landscape far, far below. It was almost as if with my eyes I could swoop down like an eagle to a distance where my eyes could focus on a particular area, while I was actually in a stationary place high above.

I looked down on what seemed to me to be the states of Wyoming, and North and South Dakota. I thought, *I can't really tell anything looking at entire states.* So, I peered more closely. I saw a remote highway winding through a forest, and a tiny speck that looked like a car. It looked similar to what you would see from an airplane. But as I watched the car, I could see that it was a station wagon, a brown station wagon. I looked up for a moment and back down to make sure I was focusing correctly. The car belonged to a friend, Paul. He and his family were traveling east toward Chicago and cities beyond. I could tell they were laughing and enjoying the trip, talking about the Lord and singing songs.

The shock of this revelation woke me up.

Comment: I had never considered these things. I remember the Jesus' parable about the beggar Lazarus in which the rich man doomed to hell wants Jesus to send Lazarus back to warn his brothers of their impending fate (Luke 16:19–31). In my mind, once you are in Heaven, you are busy with heavenly things and earth is too far away, and a return would only cause anguish. But the Bible also says, "Wherefore seeing we also are compassed about with so great a cloud of witnesses." (Hebrews 12:1). I think that doesn't necessarily mean only angels and God Himself are watching. I have come to believe, since this dream along with other experiences, that God has His reasons for sometimes opening windows in heaven for those who have gone before—windows with views to see into our time frame to see some wonderful things.

This day, in this dream, I saw a dear family that had been on my mind, who had been instrumental in praying for my husband's salvation, and for saving my life through prayer when I nearly died several years before. After the dream, I knew they were okay—even blessed. Fifteen years later, I met one of the children who was attending the Bible college near where I was living. I was able to send the family my love and greetings—but have since lost contact again. More importantly, God was teaching me more about Himself and His Kingdom. Our prayers and blessings do not go into the air or hit the ceiling without affect. When we pray according to God's Word, He watches over it to perform it (Jeremiah 1:12). It will come to pass—maybe not in our understanding, but in His. If we diligently seek Him and His perspective, we will begin to gain understanding.

Don't Believe
Your Eyes

November 1989: spiritual warfare

I had arrived home to our house from work, early one evening. I was standing, still removing my coat and purse while greeting the children, when suddenly a huge, twelve-foot demonic-looking creature entered through our front door. As I turned to face him, I told him to leave. I stated that he wasn't welcome in our home. He just stood in the doorway with the door open and laughed at me.

This bothered me, I had addressed others like him with that kind of authority and they would react by taking a step back or cringing. I began quoting scriptures at him about how the Blood of Jesus had sanctified both my family and our home, and that he was trespassing! When I paused to inhale for another round of scriptures, he laughed even louder. This went on for several repetitions. He was utterly defying me and the Word of God! I couldn't believe it! I quickly racked my brain for some *better* scriptures. I thought, *What am I doing wrong Lord?*

In a split second, the Lord took me (in the spirit) to the outside of the house so that I could see both the front and the back of this demon at the same time. The me in the house began another round of scriptures, repeating again that he must leave because our family and our home were each sanctified by the Blood of Jesus. *Then I saw that this was indeed having a drastic affect on him.* The demon in the doorway with his back to me was only about six inches tall. He was holding up a cardboard image of what he was when he first walked in the door. With each word I spoke, he shrunk!

Hallelujah! With renewed vigor and faith, I belted out those scriptures again, expecting his demise. In just a few moments, I heard a horrific, unearthly scream as he vaporized into nothing, along with his fake cardboard image.

Comment: As I have mentioned, many years ago I had nightmares. In these, I would be chased by hideous creatures intent on my destruction. The Lord delivered me from these kinds of dreams beginning in the mid to late 70s. As the Word of God got from my head to my heart, the Lord taught me about spiritual warfare—sometimes while I was asleep. Therefore, by the time I had this dream, I already knew much about it.

For anyone who may be wondering—what scriptures does she use? I will try to give you some hints. Please keep in mind, there is no formula. It isn't the words you say, it is having the Word of God, the Bible, settled deep in your heart—knowing it is the truth above all else. When I went through difficult times, I would often read the Psalms until I fell asleep with my head on the Bible. Those were the words that would often come to mind when I had difficult dreams, and when it was time to pray when I was awake, I prayed the words that were fresh in my mind as well as those down deep in my spirit.

I believe that King David and Job went through more personal battles than anyone—except Jesus himself. I instantly recall Job's words, "I know that my Redeemer lives!" (Job 19:25). This is a shout of victory over all the power of the enemy—who must one day bow to the Name above all names. When going through personal strife I recall Job's words, "Though He slay me, yet I will trust in Him." (Job 13:15) Read the Psalms—better yet memorize some of your favorites. I taught my children Psalm 91 when they were barely in school, and it has made a tremendous impact on them. I spoke Psalm 1 over my most difficult son, each day for many months, as he was leaving for high school. God is faithful. "The Lord watches over His Word to perform it" (Jeremiah 1:12).

The Abundant Life

The Pathway

September 1990: heaven

I was standing in a very, very long line that wound back and forth slightly uphill. I couldn't see where the beginning of the line was, and I wasn't sure why we were waiting in the line. The line was filled with lots of different kinds of people. They all seemed to know someone in line, and they would stand together or chat across the way as the line bent back and forth. Everyone was happy; no one was impatient even though the line didn't seem to be moving at all.

I was standing alone. I saw familiar looking people, but I didn't know anyone's name, and they were all engaged in talking to someone. I began examining the beautiful surroundings. There was a pretty little brook that wound around next to the path. It was only about two and half feet wide, about six inches deep, with stones scattered at intervals. There were young trees growing, providing just enough shade to keep everyone comfortable as they waited. The brook itself was refreshing, its trickle comforting. There were other plants growing along the way providing a definite division between the neatly manicured path and the little brook.

It is hard to describe how the brook and path wound around each other so neatly, pleasantly and efficiently. As I looked at it, I thought how really beautiful this brook was. It was too bad no one was paying any attention to it; instead, they were busy talking to each other. The more I looked at the water, the more I was intrigued. There was no mud or sand. It was like fine pebbles on the bottom and edges so that if it wasn't for the water, it would seem almost a path itself, except for the occasional rock that would stick up above the water with a smooth, dry, flat surface. In fact, I realized the brook's route was what was so well manicured and the path wove around it.

It was so inviting I decided to step into the brook. It didn't cross my mind to take off my shoes. As I stepped in, a couple people noticed and breathed out distressingly "Oh!" Of course, this caused others to look at me standing ankle deep in the brook. However, I hardly noticed anyone's reaction because the brook was *so* delicious! It was as if light and life entered into me, and I was filled and satisfied.

I cried out to them, "The brook is the pathway! That's why it seems the line isn't moving. Step into the brook and follow it!" They all just looked at me, thinking I was crazy to get off the obvious path and do something I would probably get in trouble for. They were all content and patient to wait for the line to move. Most of them turned their backs toward me so as not to notice what I was doing though a few were watching from the corners of their eyes.

I took a few steps and the water was so wonderful, the

path so smooth and easy, but no one would follow me as I began my ascent up the winding, deliciously satisfying pathway.

Comment: The water was most definitely the "living water" which flows from the throne of God. I tasted it with my feet. I think these were all good people who loved God and were on their last trek toward entering heaven. There was no evil or mistrust; it was a wonderful family atmosphere. It still grieves me, as I remember how they just wouldn't listen to me. Over the years, everyone has times when the church doesn't receive their revelation; no matter how certain they are that it is from God. I have had some bad experiences and some enlightening experiences while attending many different churches. We moved a lot, so it was hard to get established and gain trust without the Lord Himself speaking to the leadership at each church. Still, He is Faithful!

He will always find a way to get through to His people eventually. I have had a difficult time not judging others who perhaps don't recognize the hand or voice of God, as quickly as I do. I have become frustrated and had to learn the patience of Job, which is really the patience of God. Even if I didn't move ahead of the others in that line and had only stood in the same place, it would be more refreshing and fulfilling to stand in the "living water" while waiting. Others just don't see sometimes. And it never occurred to me to bend down and take a sip. This is humbling to me—why was I satisfied with this new revelation without seeking more? I was not smarter or better because I happened to receive the revelation about the true path. Just like the others, I was satisfied with my level of revelation at the time. We need to continually pray for Revelation, both for ourselves and for each other. We all see through a glass darkly (1 Corinthians 13:12) and need God's perspective.

Heavenly Procession

April 1991: heaven

I was walking on a sort of cobblestone street. There were no vehicles, only people walking. The sidewalk was narrow and full of people hustling back and forth. The buildings were tall and made of stone. There were small shops with shopkeepers that seemed to know and greet every person that walked by. I was headed to a shop on the left side of the street almost at the corner. I looked down at the stone street. They were very unusual stones. They kind of glistened and were transparent, yet they were just stones in the street—not gems or jewels.

I stepped onto the sidewalk as a commotion began in the street. Everyone in the street and in the shops came pouring out into the street all at once. But instead of a din of voices, at the same time all grew quiet and listened. I could hear faintly, and coming nearer the jangling of horses and a voice singing. In fact, as the sound grew louder it was apparent that a small entourage was approaching. The jangles were not just from the horses, but the sound of tiny cymbals and other simple instruments were playing. The voices were singing an announcement of the approach.

"Behold! Behold! Behold the Gift of God!"

I never saw the covered carriage, if it was a carriage. In my imagination, I could see it approaching the intersection and turning the corner to come exactly where I was. The people were already peering, leaning forward, and anticipating the moment when they would see the King.

Comment: I never liked parades. They seem silly to me, so it was strange that I would have such a dream. The catchy tune ran through my head for many months afterward. I've yet to hear worship, even spontaneous worship, which has played this heavenly tune. It has been many years, yet I know I will recognize it when I hear it—though I can no longer hum it.

Even during the dream, I knew I was in a heavenly setting. I had an errand that had to be completed, as did most of the others in the dream. But everything gets put on hold when you get the opportunity to spend some time with the King of Kings. The thing that impressed me most was the glorious anticipation that each person had. They didn't go rushing toward the sound. They waited patiently, as if waiting for their turn, to enjoy His presence. They were all kinds of people, but they were all gentle and friendly, not like any town or city I have ever encountered. The very atmosphere of the place made you know you were in a heavenly place, more than what you actually saw or experienced. It felt *wonderful*.

Future Son-in-Law

January 1995: prophetic

I don't remember most of the dream. I do remember sitting in a church with my family and several pews ahead of us was a young man with dark hair. We were in a church that was unfamiliar to me. It felt as if we were visitors, yet we had been there before. I seemed to know some of the people, but most were strangers. I felt the Lord had spoken to me and said he was the young man who would one day marry my daughter. I was sure it was God who had spoken to me.

So I began fidgeting trying to get a better look at who this was, but I could only see the back of his head. His hair was cut rather short, and looked black or very dark brown, from the distance we were at.

Comment: I don't recall anymore of the dream, though I know there was more. I include it here because shortly after this dream, my daughter announced her engagement. But it was to a young man with light blond hair. This was upsetting to me, because I really felt the dream was from God—but I hadn't had the opportunity to share it with her. The young man was a model student and in leadership at his church. He seemed really nice and they had known each other for a few years. I really wanted her to be happy. So, I supported her and prayed asking God what all this meant.

As they got to know each other in this new light of being engaged, some issues came up in their relationship. It began to be apparent that this was not the person she was to marry. I just kept praying, still keeping the dream in my heart. I shared it only with my closest prayer partner. My daughter broke off the engagement after a few months and it was very hard on her—him too. So, I still did not share the dream with her.

A while later she began dating a guy from work. My daughter and I worked at the same company, so I also knew him a little as a co-worker. He was really nice—but I didn't know if he was a Christian. So, I went back to my knees. "Lord, this guy has black hair, but is he the husband I have been praying for my daughter for since she was a little girl?" As I got to know this young man better, I became more accustomed to their being together. At least there was no check in my spirit, but God did not directly answer my question, I had to trust Him.

This young man did ask her to marry him some time later—very romantically. As she shared the experience with us, I knew inside that it was meant to be. This was God's confirmation. I finally shared the dream with her. He has turned out to be the best son-in-law I could ever ask for. I often see the back of his head and am reminded that it wasn't their choosing, but God's that they would be married and serve God together, active in their church and blessing all of us with their children.

The Frozen Mountain Top

April 1995: heaven, airplane

I seemed to be trapped with some other people in the body of an airplane. The plane had crashed and was partially submerged in the freezing waters of a stream near the top of a jagged, frozen mountain. Some of the people were slumped over in their seats, dead or asleep—either from the impact or from the cold. Some of the people were moving back and forth. There was no exit toward the cockpit, no exit toward the back of the plane. If we were to open an emergency door over where the wings used to be, it would let in more of the frigid water.

The floor was gradually filling with water. There seemed to be no hope. Some looked toward those who were unconscious with some envy. We had been in that position only minutes; rescue would take days. There was literally no hope for survival. Those unhurt would quickly freeze to death.

The scene changed, and I saw a large group of people sitting in a makeshift circle. We were in a warm place; it was twilight. I realized that some of those in this circle were some of the same people that had been on the plane. They were taking turns telling of their experiences, how they had died. I was in heaven. The people were laughing and joking. There was no fear, and it wasn't awful to speak about dying. We had all already done it. As others began to tell their stories, I realized that as they spoke it was as if you were in a 3D movie or something. This gave you the ability to experience their death along with them. It seemed important that we all described how we got there. Then, we could move on. I thought, if we can experience each other's death this way, we should be able to share in each other's joys as well.

Comment: When I woke up, I first thought that I had died in the plane crash, but as the rest of the dream ran through my mind, I thought that perhaps that wasn't how I got there. I wasn't one of those sharing. It was the people on the other side of the circle. I was listening, or I should say, observing.

It strikes me that our perspective is going to be so different once we get to heaven that we cannot even imagine what our memories of earth will be. Tears and sorrows are wiped away, yet we remember and even recognize people we have never seen. That is so far beyond our comprehension. Jesus has taken untold thousands by the hand and led them into eternity despite horrendous circumstances. Yet the glorious communion, or union, with Him completely overshadows the circumstance, the pain, or the fear. Dying isn't the worst thing that can happen to you—sometimes living is!

All this, of course, assumes you know Jesus as your Lord and Savior. I know how I was tormented as a child, with the fears I once had of the demonic beings that at times wouldn't leave me alone. I cannot imagine for a second how horrible hell would be. There demons are tortured, and in their hatred of God, and man who is made in His image, they would torture people who chose to turn away from God. God have mercy.

Newborn Babies

September 1995: prophetic

I had several dreams in the past couple years about giving birth. The children are usually girls, and though they are newborns, they can sit up, sometimes even walk and talk! The one I remember best is where I am in the hospital, wondering where the father is because I am about to give birth. Suddenly, it's all over and the nurse is bringing me a child. I am ready to take the helpless infant into my arms to nurse it, it has clothes on, and, it is no longer a newborn. I am still in the hospital bed recovering from the birth, and they have to close the door so my child doesn't run out into the hallway!

In one dream like this, I had a Cesarean birth (C-section). I was not moving for fear of causing myself pain from the incision, but when I saw the child talking to the nurse, I lifted the covers and found my stomach was healed and totally normal!

Each time I have one of these dreams, I am aware that this is just not normal—so I must be dreaming. I remembered in my dream that I had had my tubes tied many years before, so this had to be a miracle baby—and it was. This baby could sit up at birth, and as the minutes past, it was as though months—then years passed. The child appeared to be nearly five years old when it was time to leave the hospital a few hours after she was born.

Comment: I had this kind of dream only for a couple years—years when I wasn't married. As I mentioned, my tubes were tied. I was wondering if God would restore some of the years the locust had eaten by giving me a godly husband and children again to keep me young. But I realized even then, that they were probably spiritual children. I wasn't involved with children's ministry, and I didn't even have a Bible study then.

I have never felt I had the calling to be an evangelist—I am usually an encourager to the body of Christ. But I have shared many stories about God's grace and goodness in my life—through some really difficult things. Even unbelievers want to hear more. So perhaps I have had some unknown children along the way. Recently, I had another one of these dreams. The number fifty-five was in the dream—thank God for His mercy and grace! The number five usually indicates grace—here, double grace.

I now understand that babies can indicate a birthing of a something planned or initiated by God. Female babies (which these were) speak of the fruit as the outcome of handling an assignment by God, as promised. New projects, ministries or ventures can be depicted as babies, indicating their small beginnings but ultimate success. I believe God has been preparing me for new great and mighty ministry, which I hadn't even conceived of. The quick maturing means that the fruitfulness of the ministry will come speedily. Our ministry is still in its infancy, and we have been praying about what God wants us to do next. Recalling these dreams gives assurance that we have been executing God's plan and that He will continue to prosper all we put our hand to, as in Psalms 1.

A Different View of Our World

May 1996: end times

I am driving in a large vehicle. I can't tell if it's truck or van, though the compartment is large. I am so intent on what I am experiencing, I don't take the time to look in the mirror, let alone look into the backseat. The dashboard is dark brown; the seats are a lighter tan color. I look at the gauges again and again. The speedometer doesn't work. The gas gauge is apparently broken, or we are driving without gas. Even the steering had the feel that I was barely in control.

It seems I am with my children—or some of them. We are driving alone on roads, traveling across country. We pass wide-open spaces with occasional signs of a town or small city in the near distance. There is a sense of urgency to get somewhere and a sense that we are living a miracle. There is no other traffic, and I had to look way ahead for obstructions in the road or missing bridges. I had the sense that there were no working vehicles, I also assumed there was no gas that could be purchased and if someone thought we had some, we were sure to be questioned—or have it forcefully taken from us.

I kept driving; everyone was peering out the windows looking for danger. We didn't speak, we were praying intently and silently. Every mile, every inch, was a miracle bringing us closer to the destination.

Comment: I have had similar dreams many times over the past 30 years, and usually I remember only bits and pieces. Each has the same feeling of having survived to a time when everything in America is very different. It is as if a disaster that would affect the entire country had occurred. There is always a sense of danger, a sense of secrecy, a sense that we were living in the miraculous. It would probably behoove us to take these things into account in our daily lives. How many times have we been called *the Army of the Lord*? We don't often act like soldiers engaged in a war. I have been reminded by my two sons who served in the US Army from 2001–2005, that a soldier is a soldier 24 hours a day, 365 days a year—always on alert, always on call, always on duty—even when on leave.

These dreams and what I understand through reading the Bible, lead me to believe that there will always be those of us who survive the most difficult and devastating events that could possibly occur on this earth. This would include natural disasters and unimaginable military attacks just the same. After reading testimonies of people who have survived being in the midst of the twin towers collapsing and the ravages of Hurricane Katrina and reading about the modern day martyrs particularly in Muslim countries today, I cannot see God abandoning this world. He will always have His remnant walking this planet. They will continue to speak His Word and see His Will and Purpose accomplished.

Flying Lessons?

February 1997: heaven, prophetic

I was taken to a large hanger or warehouse-type building by an angel. This angel looked much like a human, a little taller perhaps. However, I still knew it was an angel that was instructing me. We entered through a regular doorway into a vast area. The building was completely empty. At the far end were some others, angels with people, probably there for the same reason.

I knew I was to receive instruction, but I couldn't imagine what it might be as the place was so empty and rather dimly lit. I stood, indicating I was ready. I looked up at the ceiling; it was probably four stories high. The angel said, "Jump." Well, I didn't really think about why I might be jumping, but when an instructing angel tells you to do something, you just do it. I jumped, with a sincere amount of effort.

I was quite surprised when I realized I had managed to jump several feet off the ground. I landed and steadied myself. As I did, the angel, of course, said, "Jump again." So I did, trying harder this time to see if I could get higher.

I did! I probably jumped to fifteen feet easily. I had to prepare to land on my feet, and I realized somehow that if I looked up, my feet would instinctively do the right thing so I could land solidly, ready for another jump. This I did several times, each time getting closer to the ceiling. Finally, on the last jump, I knew that it was only the ceiling restricting me from going higher. I had to gauge myself so as not to bang my head. It was an exhilarating feeling, like when you do rock climbing and you actually make it to the top.

That was all. I knew that I had completed my lesson for the day and done well. I woke up satisfied.

Comment: This dream has kind of puzzled me. I know for certain the angel was instructing me. They don't use a lot of words, but they are really teaching more than it appears. I could figure it all out myself by just doing what they said. I guess you would describe it as though it was a slow motion thing where they guide your movements so quickly that it seemed as though I was simply jumping and landing. However, the angel probably did a lot of guidance and correction, imperceptivity to me. But I did learn. My body absorbed the instruction, sort of bypassing the mind.

Why jumping in a warehouse? I don't know. It was a sort of basic training I think. I had the impression that somehow I was being trained in the possibilities of the *new body*. To me, I was the same, but I wasn't and didn't realize it. I guess that is true with all of us as we grow in our walk with the Lord. We are always capable of much more than we think. We just have to be obedient and trust God to do the rest.

The warehouse could have represented the traditional churches I had been associated with. My unknown ability and the exercise I did to reach higher heights *inside* the confines of the church was a revelation to me. In 1997, God had placed me into a large church where I questioned how I was going to be a useful or relevant part. It is almost like the Lord was telling me then that I could do some spiritual soaring within the place and that He would eventually launch me from that place, once I had learned some techniques. The Lord would be my teacher and use the setting and opportunities in that church to prepare me for the next level.

Blessed Assurance

February 1997: end times

I was floating up through the sky. I say floating because I thought I was on an airplane, but there was no airplane. I looked around me and could see clouds in every direction. Some were distant; some were close. I didn't look down, but I had the sense that I was twenty thousand feet up or more. Suddenly, I heard a voice calling to me from the western sky. Very far off in the distance I could just make out a person waving at me. I could hear a voice shouting, "Hey, Mom, over here, it's me!" The voice was very faint because of the great distance, but it was unmistakable. It was my son, Stewart.

Comment: I really don't recall much of this dream, but the part I do remember has come to my memory over and over again. I know it was from God.

I don't believe in rapture, at least not the way it is depicted by Tim LaHaye, Hal Lindsey, and the like. So it did not cross my mind while I was floating up that this was that. In fact, my son and I seemed to be the only ones in the sky. Although the sky is pretty big, I know there would have been other believers between us. He seemed several states away—hundreds of miles. What I did get from the dream was God's absolute assurance of His keeping power. I knew from that moment forward that my son would never stray from God. Though I may not see him, I could know for certain that he would be there, on the same spiritual plane as I am, secure in His relationship with God, and secure in God's protection. It was he, keeping an eye on me and letting me know he was there, and we were both going up!

My son was a senior in high school when I had this dream. Little did I know that he would be miraculously going off to college in Missouri for four years (we lived in New York State). Then, he would immediately go into the Army for four years, to Germany and then to Iraq. By the time, he came home, I had moved to Israel. This dream, and another supernatural intervention of God that happened four years later, gave me the assurance I would need as a mom, to walk in perfect peace, which passes all understanding through all of his travels. I'm still walking in this today, Praise God!

Underground Caves with Neptune Men

April 1997: spiritual warfare

I was walking downward through a dimly lit cavern. There were paths leading up and down and some went off into adjoining caverns. I was on a main pathway, but it wasn't very traveled as it was very deep. I was with a companion. I didn't look at the person, but I knew there was someone with me. We finally reached the bottom where there was some piping like a place of waterworks. Bluish pipes rose out of the small pool of black water. The water may have been clear, and just appeared black because of the lack of real light. There were torches on the walls, you could see easily, but it was that yellow kind of light.

I walked right up to the pipes and sort of pumping station. I touched it as I leaned to examine the pipes coming up out of the water as if inspecting them. Then, suddenly it was time to leave. I was hurried along, and we kept looking behind us to see if we were seen, or were being followed. We passed a few people on the way down, and now we also passed them on the way up. They all traveled on the trails leading up. They all looked like zombies, staring straight ahead as they plodded along. I wondered who would ever even notice us. But we hurried up the increasingly steep passageway.

Soon there was some shouting behind us and on the opposite side of the cavern wall that was our pathway. I looked, and thankfully, there was a pit between us, creating two separate paths. These creatures were shaped much like men, but they looked kind of slimy like the skin of a salamander. They wore no clothing and they had tails. They shouted in some strange language while pointing at me and threatened me with their spears. The spears were long thin poles of metal with three pronged points at the end. They were about three to four feet long and the prongs were about four inches long and wide.

I decided to ignore them. Then, as I took a step, they began throwing the spears at me. This irritated me, and at first, I threw a couple back at them. Their tails seemed to help them balance to be better at throwing the spears, which made them much more accurate than I. I realized that they only had a few spears so giving them back only helped them, while doing so was slowing me down. The spears clanked all around me as I tried to run up the steep passageway to get away from them. Their sound faded as I ascended.

Comment: I realized when I first had this dream that it was about spiritual warfare. There was some secret thing that I needed not only to see, but also to experience and understand way down at the bottom. It was dangerous, but I was in God's care. He even gave me wisdom about not enabling the enemy, but to press on to the task at hand. I understood the *Neptune men* (which I began to call them) to be demons that were not very powerful, at least in this appearance. Yet they had been given this important task because it was unlikely they would have an encounter so deep and close to their place of abode.

I now understand that caverns like this usually indicate a prophetic birthing, like a womb. There was water, but it was so deep that it had to have a means to bring it to the surface. The pipes were a unique color blue, indicating their heavenly origin. I think there is a deep spiritual message that the Lord sent me to examine and help bring to the surface. It would seem I have prophetic knowledge that will flow when God opens the valves. The *Neptune men* were demonic figures that represent false prophets. They had tails making me believe they represented the sensual aspect, which has come against me most aggressively in the past. They may oppose, but they are not effective in hindering the delivery of God's Word and purpose.

On a Bridge

July 1997: end times, spiritual warfare

I found myself walking on a bridge that appeared to be a highway above the streets through a major city. I had the impression it was New York City, but it seemed strange. The city was dark and quiet though it was still daylight. There were no cars, and it seemed as though there was no traffic movement anywhere in the city. All was strangely silent for such a large city with towering high rises and tall buildings in the immediate vicinity. I stood still, looking at the surroundings in wonder. It was a two-lane road in one direction, with an on-ramp next to me.

I saw a couple walking up the on-ramp. They were engaged in a conversation, talking intently, walking close together, and speaking in hushed tones. I then noticed other people scattered around in small groups of two or three walking briskly about their business, or more slowly, in a hushed manner. No one was concerned with the possibility of traffic on the roads—there was no traffic at all.

Suddenly I saw a dark figure walking up the same ramp. He

was about thirty feet behind the couple, and they were unaware of him. He was looking at them intently. He didn't seem to notice me or anything else. He was pacing himself, concentrating on the couple, gaining on them step by step so they wouldn't even notice. But I sensed that he was about to attack them.

I wanted to intervene and direct the couple's attention to this suspicious man. I was on the inside lane of the two lanes, and the people were on the far side of the ramp—almost three lanes away from me. As I took a step in the direction of the ramp, the dark figure decided to make his move. I realized in a split second that this was no man, or if a man—he was demonically possessed, as he seemed to leap in the air from about fifteen feet away from them. I shouted directly at him. "Die! In the Name of Jesus!"

Instantly, in mid-air, he let out a blood-curdling screech that seemed to echo between the buildings. It was as if he hit an invisible wall. A puff of dark smoke appeared, and he vanished from the spot in the air where he had leapt. There was a mass of black clothing in a pile just below the spot. I was horrified! I thought that I had perhaps killed someone. I couldn't even tell for sure if there was a body in the crumpled mess of cloth.

I awoke with my heart beating hard—not fast, just hard. It really disturbed me that I had killed the creature, even though I felt I had literally saved two people's lives. It disturbed me that I had said such words.

Comment: At the time I experienced this dream, the Lord had taught me a lot about spiritual warfare and the very real attacks of the enemy against the body of Christ. I had studied Ephesians 6 about putting on the full armor of God and had learned of the power in the Blood of Jesus and in the Name of Jesus though I had always had the perspective of being on the defensive, doing just enough to save souls and at the same time doing damage to the enemy's plans, but, to me, this was on par with Jesus casting out demons to utter darkness. I have enough understanding to know that you don't do these kinds of things unless directed by the Holy Spirit. Never out-step your authority. I hadn't considered that demons often use men as their hosts or thought about what happens to that man when you deal with these most terrible sorts of demons. God has a special love for his creation—man.

We must have His perspective on *all* things, at *all* times. In the flash of an instant, we may be faced with making these kinds of life and death decisions. We cannot be prepared except for diligently seeking God on a daily basis to stay in sync with Him. But we cannot hesitate; we must be able to trust God with the details. Was there a man in the clothing? Was he now dead? I woke up, so I couldn't find out, or do, anything. Perhaps the very ones whose lives were in danger would be the ones to nurse the man back to wholeness after the demon left, or they would be the ones to deliver his body to his family or the authorities. We must be able to trust God and handle only those things He gives us. That doesn't mean we are looking for someone else to do the *dirty work*. God looks for our obedience. He will give us what we need to accomplish His purposes—even miraculously.

Angels Help Building

January 1998: prophetic, angels

I saw two huge angels standing amidst the walls going up for the new sanctuary at our church. They were three or four stories high. I stared at them in wonder; I had never imagined such huge angels. The building, or the walls that would become the building, were being raised up. The floor was poured concrete, and there were foundational pieces jutting up from the ground here and there. Two main walls were still only a few feet high, but the other two, toward the streets, were almost full height. There were workers moving back and forth, some working on the walls, some on other things. I could see that many were contractors, not members of the church. Somehow, I knew that most of those were not believers. The angels were each holding up a wall, and had their other hand at the ready, on their swords. The workers were oblivious to the angels, although some believers were worshipping in the Spirit as they did their work.

The angels themselves were dressed in what I would

describe as military dress uniform. For an angel, this is a white tunic with a gold sash around the waist and going up to one shoulder. A sword with gold trim hung at one side. There was some sort of gold trim around their heads too. Their hair was brown, but not long and flowing as feminine angels are often pictured. The angels were masculine, very powerful and authoritative looking. They appeared to be some of the host of the Lord's Army at their best. It was surprising to me that such an angel would be involved in construction, and here were two of them!

Comment: When I awoke, I immediately was reminded of Nehemiah and how he had instructed the Israelites in rebuilding the walls to carry their swords. But, this was the city of Rochester, New York, so it was obviously spiritual forces that were the danger. It is interesting that at the time, the walls were not yet at this stage. I saw them but had no idea how tall they would be, or what they would look like. Several weeks later when the walls were raised, it was apparent I saw them correctly. The other thing that impressed me immediately about this dream was as I asked the Lord about this, He said, "As the physical walls are built they will reflect the spiritual building of my church in this city." The church was building by faith, as the funds came in. Our pastor's vision was for the structure to be shared by the *church* in Rochester, and not just for our congregation. He had spent years developing relationships and praying with pastors in the surrounding areas. Now God himself was overseeing the building of His church.

This dream also had meaning for me personally. I prefer small, country churches where you feel at home, like a family. Our existing church was already too big for me. Yet it was busting out at the seams, and God had clearly sent me there. On several occasions, I had to sit on the stairs to the balcony—there was standing room only in the services. This was a strong confirmation to me that God was the one who wanted a bigger sanctuary; His blessing was upon not only the building but also the vision.

Banqueting Tables

May 1998: heaven

I was in a huge banquet hall. Before me were rows of long, long tables. I was standing at the beginning of the first table. It was set beautifully with nice tablecloths and the best silverware, goblets, and plates. Every detail was beautifully complete. The centerpieces were wonderful candelabras and even the high back chairs went with the decor. There were angelic servants rushing back and forth, placing the finishing touches on the settings of all the tables.

There were many rows of tables. Each table stretched farther than I could see from where I stood. Each row was set differently. I went to the next table, and it was lavishly set. It had gold utensils and crystal goblets with many of them at each place setting. It looked like it would if you were expecting royalty. The chairs were of velvet and plush. It was breathtaking—yet I would be nervous at that table, for fear of breaking something, and I never know what to do with all the silverware and glasses.

I walked between the tables looking at each one's personality. One was a simple table. It had basic wooden chairs and simple place settings. It was still very nice, just a humble setting. There was everything in between. There must have been twenty rows or more of these different place settings. Each time I looked at the table, I would picture the type of people that would sit there. They would be so happy and blessed at such a setting and such a feast!

As I saw the people in my mind, I realized that they did not look around at the other people's tables. Each one assumed that all the tables were just as elegant as theirs, and that they all were equally blessed. What an amazing feat the Host had accomplished with such a design! I looked at the angels scurrying about. They were very serious about their work, and yet there was an anticipation of joy. They knew their work was to bless not only the people but also the Master, and, it was important that every detail was just right.

Comment: Several things about this dream are important to me. First, the banquet setting was almost complete! This dream was in 1998, if the banquet table in heaven is almost complete, surely the Lord's return cannot be far away. Second, the different settings for the people of all different statuses are significant. I didn't feel that it was only kings and dignitaries that would sit at the most elaborate table. In fact, I knew there would be some of the most lowly, humble people at that table—but they wouldn't feel, as I did, uncomfortable being there—they would belong there, and the dignitaries that ended up at a different table would feel just as honored, by the Master. There would in fact be no status, only honor. In our world, we usually perceive honor and status both together. But we can understand the concept of honor from God's perspective if we think of men of honor and integrity that we have heard of in every walk of life. For example—it could be a barefoot preacher in Africa, who is as honored and respected as a beloved leader in an advanced nation's military.

It is amazing that people would not take notice of what was happening at the other tables. We compare ourselves to others so much—always judging. Even in Job's day, his friends assumed he had some secret sin and therefore deserving of God's punishment upon him. When we truly get our eyes focused on our Lord, that kind of judging will all fall away. Praise God!

This dream also reminded me of a dream told me by an eight year-old girl. She was a sweet little girl, with a heart of gold, who loved Jesus. She was always helping her mom, people at church and anyone she met. Her family had invited ours to live with them for a couple months when ours was homeless in 1985. One day she shared a dream that she was in heaven working in the kitchen. She said she was so excited for the privilege of getting to serve Jesus! She worked hard and tried to do everything just right. Then Jesus called her to come and sit next to him at the banquet table. She started to protest, as she was only a child, but He insisted, so she wiped her hands and sat down next to Jesus. I'd love to know where this young woman is today. I am sure the Lord's hand is on her in a mighty way.

The Life Boat

February 2001: end times, prophetic

We were in a city that was flooding. The place where we were standing on was breaking apart with the wind and the waves. My youngest son was with me. We were clutching each other tightly, standing on a ledge with many people—hoping and praying for a lifeboat. Some boats floated by. They were usually over-crowded with people, and they didn't even come close to the place where we stood. If anyone were to jump into these boats, they would capsize because of too many passengers.

Suddenly a boat came near. It wasn't full, and it was being piloted by my two older sons. They had come to rescue us! All of the people standing with us got into this boat. But it was then too full and in danger of capsizing. So my two older sons jumped out of the boat. Then the boat was seaworthy. We would be able to get to safety.

The current grabbed the boat and began whisking it away. I called to my sons to hang on. If they could just hold the sides, they might be strong enough to hang on and make it. They both looked me in the eyes and said, "No mom. That won't work." Cheerfully they said, "We can find another boat; we will be all right". I knew they could not survive in that churning, dangerous water, and there were no more boats. It was a miracle they had found this last one. Time was running very short. As they were pulled away in the current in different directions, I knew I would never see them again. I held my younger son close, realizing they had given their lives for ours.

Comment: This dream brought to light for me just how my sons have learned to love, even to the point of laying down their lives for others. This was one of many ways the Lord was preparing me at the time to accept them both going into the Army the following summer. Yet at the time I had this dream, neither of them was thinking about it.

In light of the bigger picture, it also shows me that they are prepared for life and even the end-times when we will all face trials we cannot imagine at present. The Lord has settled in my heart that they will indeed be faithful to Him, to the end. That is a huge burden off a parent's shoulders. I *can* let them go, trusting that the Lord will guide them every step. Praise God.

> And all thy children shall be taught of the LORD; and great shall be the peace of thy children.
>
> Isaiah 54:13

Overcoming Faith

Caverns Filling with Water

November 2001: end times, prophetic

We were underground in caverns that were well lit and had people, shops, and streets. It seemed as though people had moved underground to live. I was walking through the cavern when there was a rumble, like an earthquake that lasted for a couple of minutes. I was with my youngest son; I held tight to his hand as this quaking occurred. People began screaming in panic and running uphill toward the exit.

    I stood still for a moment. Then, instinctively, I began heading further down into the cave. My son protested for a moment, pointing out that everyone else was running the other way. If there was going to be a collapse and the water was rising, why would we go deeper? We then encountered my other two sons who were kind of looking around, not sure which way to go. I told them that I felt God was saying, "Go deeper." They took off to check out what was ahead of us. The screams grew faint behind us as we hurried downward; no one else was headed in our direction. The water was rising; the streams that normally flowed downhill were flowing in the opposite direction.

Comments: Caves or caverns usually indicate a birthing—often a birthing of the prophetic. It is interesting that my children, at least the boys, were all with me. I sensed that we were to ignore our own sense of logic and that safety would come from obeying God's voice, even when in didn't make sense to us. The shaking and the water rising could indicate that the birth was about to take place, but it seems that it would have been an untimely birth. God's timing is perfect, but the prophetic gifting in our family had not yet matured to the place of God's release.

INORDINATE EXPECTATIONS

February 2002: *prophetic*

I was standing when I noticed there was something attached to my leg, which I couldn't seem to shake off. It wasn't heavy like a ball and chain would be, but it was persistent. I looked down and saw the most ugly, tightly twisted ball of disgusting flesh-looking stuff. It was so gross looking; it made me imagine I could smell something rotting terribly. It was larger than a basketball. *That* was what was attached to my leg, and it wouldn't come off. I was in God's presence, I don't know how I understood that, but I just asked Him, "What is it? It looks like a ganglion cyst—a growth of some sort, and it's SO disgusting!"

The Lord answered, "It is *Inordinate Expectations*".

Comment: God's words pierced my heart, as they always do, but this became a progressive revelation. I immediately understood that it was my own wrong expectations toward myself, my parents, my children, my marriages, friends—you name it, I had expectations, and they were *wrong*! It wasn't a sin that was against those people; although obviously, these things could affect relationships, but the real sin was against God—and myself. In the area of relationships, I had been very broken—ever since I was very young. This blinded me to God's perspective in this area. Here I was, the mom who had such different personalities in each of her four children that she had to interpret all the time for each of them so they could learn to understand each other. Even at my job, I excelled in interpersonal communications because I was so good at dealing with difficult personalities and helping others to understand one another. Yet my own expectation of myself—and others—was incorrect.

I was shocked and ashamed that I had messed up so badly and especially because I had been blind to the ugly growth for such a long time! However, I also knew that this wasn't an accusation from God, but a revelation, so that I could choose to begin to receive His perspective and walk in His mercy. I pleaded with God that He would change me and take this horrible thing away, but I knew that it was something I had to walk through and learn from, and as I did, I would release others and myself.

I began with my parents. I had already been through a reconciliation time, where I forgave and asked forgiveness—but that kind of fell to the side when there had been a family disagreement and my stand for righteousness was considered an attack on the family. I realized even in that, I had expected my parents to act lovingly and logically—which was not even remotely likely to happen in that situation. I had expected Christian husbands to be godly men that lived by the Bible, trusted God, and obeyed His Word. There is this little thing called *freewill*, which along with a carnal nature, will pull man down every time he gives it opportunity. These men couldn't be as strong as I thought they should be. My expectations were wrong regardless of how many times they chose sin over righteousness.

I found myself repenting again for being such an inadequate parent, this time realizing I expected too much from my children—and myself. I was always pushing, always trying to be perfect. I had to learn to let each person in my life (and even myself) go. The process went on for a couple weeks when I received a confirmation prophecy. The person said they saw me looking down at a huge, tangled mess with my hands lifted as if to say, *How can I untangle all this?* And they said the Lord was saying, "I will help you." Simple, but I needed that. I saw the ball, more like a giant ball of dirty yarn now, and it was only half the size. Again, I went through a time of self-examination, more repentance and pleading with God to take it away.

Months later there was only a small ball left—now the size of a softball. I thought perhaps the Lord would then take it away, but He let me know that in the center of it was a treasure—something worth finding and preserving. So, I again embraced patience and mercy, and waited. The Lord has really taken away so much of my judgmental attitude that I cannot explain it. I have a different perspective. I could see God's perspective in specific instances before—just as when the Spirit of God would come on Samson—but then it would be gone. I learned during that year, or more, to seek to have God's perspective in all things, at all times.

I'm still not positive I know what might be the good at the center. I think it is a gift of discerning, without judging. Kind of like being able to separate the sin from the sinner, even when the sinner is embracing the sin and quite often has the stains on them. Mercy has always been the least of my giftings. I'm more prophetic—apt to call down the fire of God. So it is a new perspective for me to really consider that we don't know what a person has been through, and what truly motivates them to sin. But, once you have God's perspective and He gives the go ahead to attack the sin and rebuke the enemy, it is much more effective, like the smart bombs they use these days in the military—precisely targeted. God wants us to seek only righteous judgment.

Calling 911

April 2002: spiritual warfare

In this dream, I was standing at the kitchen sink doing dishes at my parents' house. Looking through the window above the sink, I could see two women standing at the property line, some 150 feet away. There were a few trees along the line, just the other side of a shallow ditch, which only had water in the spring. Beyond the ditch was a large farmer's field, abandoned and overgrown with weeds—once a nice field of hay.

As I looked at them, I could hear the first woman screaming terrible things at me, shaking her fist, pointing her finger, and cursing. The words were muffled, either because she was far away and shouting into the wind or because my mind just did not receive what was being said. The other woman just listened, nodding in agreement. She seemed to be an apprentice or something. I then noticed that there was an old man standing a few feet behind them and to their right. He was bowed with age, leaning on a cane and neither did, nor said anything—just watched them.

I began shouting back at them, sensing they were witches or demonic beings. I knew they wanted to come onto the property, but they could not. The ditch was to them a deep moat they could not cross. I shouted scriptures at them and told them to leave or I would call 911—or the police. I knew that I must keep my eyes on them, and that the telephone was behind me on the wall ten feet away. I couldn't get to it without taking my eyes off them for two seconds.

Their tirade continued, increasing in strength. I knew I had to follow through with my threat to call the police. So, I grabbed the phone, looking away only briefly. When I looked back, I was surprised at what I saw. Apparently, the woman had taken a step forward when I looked away. This caused her to step into the deep moat. I could see her hanging, caught on a spike that protruded about 18 inches from the top of the pit. Her head hung down as the spike caught either her clothes or her neck, and she was limp. I thought she looked dead. Her companion, the apprentice, stared in horror and disbelief. There was no way she could even retrieve the body. That woman ran away. As I looked down for a second to dial 911 and looked up again, the old man and the dead woman had disappeared. Then, so did the pit.

Comment: This dream reminds me of the warfare that has taken place on the property at my parents' house for many, many years. The house is over two hundred years old—very old for America. I have never had opportunity to research the property. It belonged to my father's mother's family, bought by my grandfather along with a good deal of the farmland surrounding it. He sold it all off, leaving just the house and 6.5 acres for my father to purchase. My grandfather even sold the mineral rights for almost nothing, so the natural gas underneath never benefited our family.

As mentioned in the Introduction, I grew up having nightmares in that house. It was rumored to be haunted, but only *slightly*. The rare, strange occurrences never really bothered my parents. They would laugh it off, joking about friendly ghosts of relatives. They certainly didn't take my bad dreams seriously. It wasn't until I accepted the Lord as my Savior that the warfare really began. I left soon after and didn't go back much—that's another long story. I learned over the years about our authority in Jesus Name and the power in the Blood of Jesus, so my children and I could visit there without fear even though some strange things still occur while we are there.

This dream speaks to me of my authority in the family concerning this property, which I had pretty much abandoned in my mind. To me, the place is old and worthless. Not a place I would choose to live, and it would cost too much to sell it, with little return. But this dream says to me that there is significance to this property in the spiritual realm. I have some kind of responsibility to take, concerning this property, for the Kingdom of God. I await further revelation. My parents are still living there. I am thankful that we do have complete victory in Jesus' Name. The Bible says, "Touch not my anointed, do my prophets no harm" (1 Chronicles 16:22). The Lord is protecting us, and the enemy's former hold is quickly slipping.

The Mantle

November 2002: prophetic

I was walking through some underground caves with a friend. We were trying not to let anyone see us, looking down so we would catch anyone's attention. We seemed unsure how to get to where we were going. She was supposed to know, but she seemed confused by so many similar landmarks. The cavern paths were dim, but not dark. The walls, floor and ceiling were all the same color of light reddish brown. There were occasional doorways. Some were just openings, some had wooden doors.

As we walked past one of the dark wooden doors with a window in it, a man stepped out to hail us. This was the place we were looking for. As the man looked in every direction to make sure we weren't noticed, we stepped inside.

On the far side of the small, cave-type room was an obviously dead, very, very old man. He was laid on a narrow wooden table, with a mantle draped over his body. Another old man, not nearly as old but definitely over eighty, was ministering busily around the dead man. I stood and watched, while a younger man made sure the door was closed securely and the shades on the door and the single window in the same wall were pulled down. This was a very secret ceremony.

The old man removed the mantle from the dead man and prepared to place it on his own shoulders. The younger man helped him. Meanwhile I looked at my friend who had brought me here. She was peeking out the window, moving the shade just a bit. When I turned back to the old man, he had fallen to the floor. He was lying on his back, now the mantle was wrapped around him. The young man was standing staring, as tears welled in his eyes. I immediately knelt down at the top of the head of the old man and held my hands to the sides of his head. My head was almost touching his as I bent close to him. I shocked myself when I heard the words that came out of my mouth.

"Lord! Don't let the anointing be lost! Lord, give to me a double portion of this anointing!" I was beginning to sob, as I looked up toward my friend. She had apparently not noticed (or maybe she did it purposely, or without understanding), but she had let the shade up. There was a dark figure outside the window, pressed up close to see what was happening in the dimly lit room. He ran when I looked at him. She saw him too and quickly pulled the shade back down, but my heart was pierced. He had seen—the enemy will know that this has taken place.

Comment: The young woman with me reminded me of a woman at the church I attended about ten years before. She was on the music ministry team, as I was, and I had heard that she was now a church secretary. I hadn't seen her in all those years, and I never thought of her as irresponsible or simple—that was how I would describe the friend who was with me in the dream though I thought it was her during the dream. She probably represented the Holy Spirit, my companion—He's definitely unpredictable at times. The old men who both had died, were ancient. One seemed over one hundred years old, the other maybe thirty years younger. I don't know anyone like that—but to me they represented generations before mine. There is Wisdom and Knowledge that has been stored up in this type of godly men.

There is also the precious anointing. The church has yet really to tap into the previous anointings we read about in church history. They are meant to be passed on to the next generation. The secrecy was obvious, God does many things that the enemy doesn't know about—scripture tells us His ways are past finding out. Even as Jesus died on the cross, the enemy hadn't figured out it was the Father's plan all along. There is much the enemy doesn't know. C.S Lewis' book *The Screwtape Letters* gives insight to this kind of thing, but it is also God's plan sometimes to give the enemy just enough knowledge to use him to ultimately accomplish God's will. "He who sits in the heavens shall laugh, the Lord shall have them in derision" (Psalm 2:4). I didn't feel any ill toward my friend; I just wondered what the ramifications were going to be. We had really tried to be in complete secrecy.

I should probably mention the beautiful mantle itself. It was a patchwork of dark, royal, velvety colors. Not like a quilt, but pieces sewn carefully together. There was also some subtle ornamentation in gold, but it wasn't lavish looking. In fact, the mantle was obviously very, very old—but well taken care of and therefore preserved. As the second old man held it, he treated it as a treasure. The atmosphere in the room reminded me of candles and incense, but I don't remember seeing the source of the light. This would imply that the presence of God was in the room.

I also recall having the attitude of, "Why am I here?" Me, of all people. Where were those whom I would have thought would be at such an important ceremony? I never had time to process those thoughts before everything transpired. This dream was disturbing to me. What in the world is God expecting of me? I know His grace is sufficient, and I will walk in that.

The underground cave itself speaks of birthing the prophetic, as well as the mantle itself being prophetic. The dark velvety color could indicate a shift from the harsh and brutal to the calm and serene. Gentleness and mercy are gifts I often ask God for, as they are not in my nature, but I have seen that the maturing of age has brought with it calmness and softening in me.

I have not shared this dream with many people. I have received prophecy on occasion where others see a mantle being placed on me by God. In 2005, this happened as confirmation that the Lord was calling me into ministry in Uganda. Then in 2006, a woman actually gave me a *Ruth mantle* made of silk with a scripture. It isn't "...your people shall be my people, your God, my God" (Ruth 4:1), the usual scripture for me, a gentile who loves Israel. The scripture is, "The LORD recompense thy work, and a full reward be given thee of the LORD God of Israel, under whose wings thou art come to trust" (Ruth 2:12). In my dream, I asked for a double portion, not knowing what I was asking for. I am reminded that Elisha asked for this when Elijah was taken to heaven in a chariot. This awareness makes me tremble, even as I am learning to lean on the Lord and trust Him in all things.

Escaping Dark Waters

May 2003: spiritual warfare

I was in dark water with my youngest son. Instead of being the teenager he was at the time, he was a small child. I had to help him to keep swimming. The water wasn't dirty, but it was very dark. It looked cold, but it didn't really feel cold, only uncomfortable. We were headed toward a ramp similar to those they use to launch boats. But there were no boats to be seen, only people and occasional debris floating by.

I was very, very tired. I am not a good swimmer. My body density allows me to lie on the bottom of a pool but not float, so swimming and trying to help a frightened child was almost more than I had the physical strength to do. There wasn't a current, but it felt as though the water made me feel heavy, pulling me down. Finally, my foot touched bottom. With great relief, I encouraged him that he also would touch bottom soon and keep moving. I was too weak to carry him. My own legs were giving way beneath me as

I began to come out of the water, and carry my own body weight on them.

Once we were out of the water and high enough that waves or high tide wouldn't affect us, I collapsed. As I seemed to loose consciousness, I was hoping that my son would stay right with me. He must also need the rest—I was so exhausted.

Comment: I believe the child in my dream was probably a symbol of spiritual children whom the Lord has given me to raise, or a ministry the Lord has for me. Many of those I minister to are younger than I—either younger in age or in the Lord, often both. The child was not my natural son because my own sons swim like fish—they would be rescuing me. The child was frightened, but not totally panicked. He was willing to trust me to find a pathway through the "dark waters." In dreams, a male child could speak perhaps of a nation.

As often happens while ministering to others, I felt inadequate and basically incapable, but I continued on, because I had to—he was depending on me. I had to rely on God's strength and His sovereign grace because I do not have the required ability, even if my heart was full of desire to help. I may possibly have perished, had I not had someone I had to rescue.

The dark water represents the worldly pulls on us. It may even have been religion. The waters could be spiritual or church doctrine that is overwhelming to the child. You couldn't see through it clearly though it wasn't totally uncomfortable. There was debris scattered around, and there were others trying to swim or wade their way through. All the time while the water pulled you down, you had to fight. This could be a picture of how the Lord would use us in Uganda. There is a constant battle against Islam, witchcraft and worldliness. Finding and then coming up the ramp was like reaching the goal the Lord has set before us. Obtaining higher ground where His revelation brings relief. We press on, depending on Him, and He gives us the victory. If it is true victory we take no glory to ourselves, and we are happiest if we have helped another to His victory, and greater revelation of Him, as well.

I truly look forward to that time of rest.

Mahogany Door

June 2003: prophetic

As I approached the tall mahogany door of the office, I looked up at the impressive dark expanse of wood towering about six feet above my head. The door opened and was then held for me to pass. As I took a step, I glanced at the person holding the door for me. It was George W. Bush, the President of the United States.

I was shocked! But felt once I had begun, I must continue this mission. But what was it? Apparently, he thought I was someone important. I didn't even know why I was there. I walked over to a large mahogany desk and stood in front of it, gazing to my right, looking around the room in wonder. Mr. Bush exited the room indicating he would send in the people to me, and I could stand right there. The room was quite dark, and there were heavy draperies hanging from the tall windows acting as dark shades. The atmosphere was one of secrecy. I didn't have much time to take in the details because suddenly there was a person standing close by, on my right side, to assist me, and the door in front of us opened.

A person was escorted into the room to stand in front of me with a brief explanation of the reason they needed to see me. I don't recall anything they said, as my head was filled with the thoughts of "How can *I* help this kind of person?" I found myself intently answering, giving expert advice and wisdom. I don't know what I said, but the person was extremely grateful and left the room bowing and thanking me, as the next person was brought into the room. One after another, ambassadors and dignitaries came and left. Much wisdom came from my lips, I seemed to know what they needed before they asked, my words somehow bypassing my brain, but ringing with sincerity as from the heart. All of the men had the same reaction as the first one.

Once, between visitors, I leaned on the desk realizing this had been going on for quite some time, and I hadn't even moved a step, let alone set down. The person beside me seemed to touch my arm, somehow encouraging me. There were many more of these people to see and there was not much time. So I took a deep breath and the door opened for the next person to enter.

Comment: This dream shook me for a long time after I received it. I didn't tell anyone about it, because although I always have had too high expectations of myself, I fear failing. But it was a confirmation of some things spoken to me over many, many years. The Lord has a deposit in me, wisdom that is His. I am reminded of the scripture

> And when they bring you unto the synagogues, and unto magistrates, and powers, take ye no thought how or what thing ye shall answer, or what ye shall say: For the Holy Ghost shall teach you in the same hour what ye ought to say.
>
> Luke 12:11–12

The first indication I recall that God thought of me as above my current stature was in 1983. I was homeless with three children, my former husband had abandoned us two months before and some church members took us in. The church was very supportive as the Lord told me to go from New York State to Virginia to seek employment with no skills. I stayed with friends of a friend (college students). We received a ride to the apartment after service one Sunday with an elder of the church and his wife. This man drove a new Cadillac, his clothes and demeanor were that of a statesman. He did not know me, but as we drove he turned to me surprised at the news of my homelessness. He said something to the effect that he thought I was like him: affluent, successful, educated—all the things I was not at the time and had no dream of ever becoming. I couldn't respond to him. I was so shocked, but like Mary—the mother of Jesus, I kept those words and pondered them in my heart.

This happened several times over the years as the Lord gradually healed my self-esteem. By 2003, when I had this particular dream, I had already been in enough corporate circles where I was at least comfortable around such people, though not really feeling like one of them. God was stretching me, really stretching me this time—way beyond the education, the jobs I had acquired, the house I owned and the salary that allowed me to be a giver rather than the needy person I had once been.

I did understand that the helper by my side was a symbol of the Holy Spirit, who is there to guide us, giving wisdom, direction and discernment—and strength. The Bible tells us that we are a Kingdom of kings and priests, who will one day rule and reign with our Lord Jesus, but this didn't seem like something that would take place someday in heaven—the fact that it was the current president tells me that it is a current possibility. So with fear and trembling and in deep humility because I am not capable, even as I felt in the dream, I prayerfully submit to God's call. I am God's willing vessel, willing to be a fool or even die, for whatever He asks of me.

Again, as Mary did, I thought, "Be it unto me according to thy word" (Luke 1:38). With a huge "Help me Jesus!" under my breath, I go forward. This is the place where I find myself everyday—in desperate need of Jesus.

An Outhouse

June 2003: prophetic

I hardly remember the first part of the dream–there were several people sitting in groups. It was a small room or compartment, like on a train or subway car. The people all seemed to know each other well. Some were sitting very close and chatting, as there was seating for only about half the people—the rest just squeezed in. I recognized some that I knew were Christians (though I don't really know them in real life). There were two different groups I mingled with, where I was attempting to get the attention of someone and to join the group. My attempt to gain attention appeared to them as a sort of a flirtation or seduction (but I didn't realize until later that it might be considered that way). They weren't interested, and I gave up, walked away, and forgot about them.

Suddenly I found myself heading for a rather large, fancy but broken down outhouse. I walked into a rather large building and began looking through the rooms for a stall of sorts. It was empty. I ended up walking out through the missing back wall. Across the street, I saw my parents' house with a nice, normal outhouse in the backyard—but I figured I was already here and there's was a long walk. I turned around and headed in another direction. Finally in a hidden area way back in the structure were several doors (apparently to stalls). But it was a small area, with low ceilings and had cheap fake flowers and vines, in an attempt to decorate it. I thought it was really strange for an "outhouse."

Comment: Shame and bewilderment were my predominant feelings during this dream. I was first misunderstood and rejected by those with whom I had hoped to be friendly. In the second part of the dream, I was looking for the toilet in the outhouse, normally they are pretty much the only thing in the outhouse. Seeing the feeble attempts to decorate a smelly, nasty place also caused bewilderment. All this reminded me of my own subconscious desire to cover up my past and my inability to remember any details. Like plastic flowers, I feel I have covered some of the unpleasantness of my childhood with amnesia. It is significant to me that I rejected going to the *nicer* outhouse at my parent's house. All these feelings make me think that there is something in my past, abuse of some sort that I have not yet dealt with. I don't want to return to the place where I feel uncomfortable. I know that God will heal me, both physically and emotionally, in His time. Sometimes it means going to places where we are humbled. It is not comfortable and we may feel shame or bewilderment. But it is the Lord's desire to heal our past so that He can use us and equip us for our future service to him.

God did not completely heal me at this time, but I understood that the process was beginning and that He would gently, gradually lead me through the entire process. He removes our shame, and if we trust Him, we don't have to remain in a bewildered state. He will lead and guide us even as he strengthens us and equips us, making all things work together for our good and God's glory (Romans 8:28).

Heavenly Gems

July 2003: provision

I was kneeling in prayer on the floor at the back of a church, during worship. It was the sanctuary of a church I had never been in before. My eyes were closed as I worshipped in the flow of the Spirit with the rest of the congregation. As I sat on my feet and lifted my head from the floor, I opened my eyes slightly. Lying on the dark royal blue carpet in front of me were a couple of tiny sparkling gems.

I blinked, to make sure my eyes weren't fooling me. Maybe the tears in my eyes caught the light to trick me. But as my eyes came into better focus, I saw even more of the tiny gems. They were cut stones, diamonds, rubies and emeralds. There were enough to gather together and pick up a small handful. As I gathered them, I looked for a basket or something to put them in. All I could see was a small hat on a table along the wall behind me. Still on my knees, I grabbed it and poured the gems into it.

Amazed at what was happening, I looked back to the place I had been kneeling. There were lots more gems. I could see that they were cut in different shapes. I especially noticed some of the rubies that were in heart shapes. I felt I had to hurry and gather up the gems quickly because the window of opportunity was short. I picked up handful after handful. As I placed them in the hat, more seemed to appear. Someone handed me another hat, and I filled a couple small hats with gems, before they suddenly stopped appearing.

Comment: This was a wonderful dream for me. I had recently had an experience of seeing my first bit of gold fleck appear on my hand in church during a teaching on Isaiah 62. I saved those first two specks and still have them in my Bible. I have seen gold dust on rare occasions since then. It reminds me of when I was a child, my aunt loved to kiss us when she greeted us, and she always had on red lipstick. So, you knew right where she kissed you on the cheek. To me it is like that, when God's presence touches you sometimes. But I wasn't into looking for gold dust or any sign—unless God specifically told me to, which He didn't.

It is interesting to me that the stones were cut. They were cut into different shapes. Each one was exquisitely beautiful as they caught the light. It is also interesting to me that they were those three types of gems: diamonds, emeralds, and rubies. To me they represent the *precious stones* mentioned in the Bible. They symbolize great wealth and prosperity, materially and spiritually. But they were at the back of the church, not at the altar. These treasures were unnoticed by anyone else in the church. Had I not been on my face, I would not have seen them, and they would have gone unnoticed completely. I believe these represent God's gift of miraculous provision, and His positioning of me.

My husband believes that because I found them at the back of the church they probably represent the more practical kinds of blessings. To me, it is significant because I like to stand at the back of the church and worship. I used to be in worship ministry, or sit on the front row, *closest to the anointing*. This is where you would normally expect to see the supernatural manifestations. Then my perspective changed, and I wanted to pull the anointing to the back of the church, so those that kind of hide or feel unworthy would also encounter that sweet, intense, wonderful presence of God.

A Visit from the King

August 2003: servants, houses

I gazed at my surroundings in wonder. *How did I get here, and where could this be?* I was at the edge of a wooded area. The road was dirt, rarely traveled by any sort of vehicle. There appeared to be several houses clumped loosely together. I was on a path toward the first house in the group.

As I walked through the old rickety wooden door and into the house, I was greeted with dirt floors and very meager surroundings. It appeared to be a hut, rather than a house. It seemed I had stepped back in time to about the fourteenth century. All of the furnishings and utensils were wooden and hastily handcrafted for utility not looks. The place was dirty, not because of neglect, but there would be no way to keep such a place clean to our standards today. I stood just inside the door finally noticing there were a couple of people working near the fireplace in the dimly lit, single room of a house. It appeared to be a mother and her young son dressed in filthy rags. Suddenly a couple of pigs came storming through the door running around my feet and the legs of the furniture before running back out the door again in an apparent "catch me if you can" game of some sort. The people looked up and chuckled at the silly pigs. They didn't seem to notice me standing in the room.

I heard a noise outside and peered out the window. Just down the road was a small entourage that appeared very strange in such humble surroundings. It was a fancy coach with nice horses pulling it accompanied by a couple of courtiers. I turned to look at the people in the house to see how they would react to the commotion outside. They continued with their work. They were busily crafting something as though some everyday task. They sat on simple stools close to the dim light of the small fire in the fireplace.

Suddenly there was a knock on the door. One of the residents got up to answer the door. I stepped aside. The door opened from the outside as they approached it. Standing in the doorway was a man dressed in kingly apparel. The colors of the royal robes were dark; the material looked like a velvet of sorts. This stately gentleman was not at all taken aback by the meager home and its furnishings. He smiled the warmest most welcoming smile as he looked at these humble people who bowed at his appearance. He had come to speak blessings to them and sincere thanks for their faithful service.

I was so impressed that this king had come to this tiny town. I wondered if the pigs would come again, but I also sensed that he would chuckle as this family did. I was impressed that he even knew this town existed with a huge kingdom to keep track of. His smile was so warm and generous as if he were a relative come to visit, not a noble who was obviously not related. I was also impressed with the love the people felt for him at his appearance. They were content with their meager, humble lives in service to their king. His greeting and blessing were more than enough reward for their hard work and difficult lives. As I turned to get a better look at this amazing king, I awoke.

Comment: I think this is a beautiful illustration of our Lord's love for us as his servants. We really do not understand the majesty, beauty, and holiness that He is. Nor do we grasp His love for us as we humbly live for Him. All our riches are as filthy rags, yet when He looks upon our filth He sees only loving, faithful servants.

You see, to God, the richest palace on this earth, with all the most beautiful paintings, furnishings and expensive ornaments and gadgets, would appear to Him to be just a humble, dirty, meagerly furnished hut from a backwards, dark age. Yet the faith filled love and obedience of His humble servants is like refined gold. How it blesses His heart when he looks upon us and sees His own reflection in us. Selah. Take some time and think about these things. I believe the Holy Spirit will speak to you too.

Gold Bar

August 2003: provision

I saw a very old locomotive slowly pulling a single flat car. The train was rolling on very old, rusty tracks that apparently had not been used in many, many years. When I looked at the flat car, I saw an enormous bar of gold. It was a single bar as large as the flat car itself. I hardly had time to gasp at the wonder of it, as the person standing next to me, my dear friend Jeanine, exclaimed, "Look at that old train! How can it move on such rusty old tracks?" I laughed at the sound of her voice and her unique perspective and woke up.

Comment: I believed this dream was for my good friend Jeanine who is in full-time ministry. That's what the train symbolized. I was to attend a going away party for her the next day. The gold bar stands for extreme abundance of provision. In the dream, she wasn't impressed as much with the amount God provided but with how He had done it in such a surprising, unlikely way.

When I shared the dream with her, another friend had

an interpretation that was similar, but added that God was going to use her as a conduit—perhaps an unlikely conduit—of His blessings to others. She said that God had positioned Jeanine to distribute to others in need, individuals, and ministries in Israel. I heartily agreed.

Today, my husband and I are one of those ministries in Israel that could potentially receive some of that provision. In 2003, a husband or full-time ministry would have been a distant dream for me. I am reminded that our dreams are usually for ourselves. Wouldn't it be a wonderful twist if God meant for us to be part of the provision or part of the recipients. All I can say is, "Do it Lord!" Praise and Glory be to God!

Deep Calls unto Deep

Angel over Western Wall, Jerusalem

September 2003: angels, prophetic

I was standing at the Kotel area (sometimes called the Western Wall) in the Old City of Jerusalem. I heard the sound of a shofar and instinctively looked up. I saw a huge angel, much bigger than I had ever even imagined an angel could be. This angel stood on top of the wall. One foot was at each end of the area above where Jews and Christians often visit for prayer. The angel had to be more than a hundred feet tall, as the stride looked proportionate to the height of the angel. The angel was wearing a long white robe with a golden sash. The clothing wasn't ornate, yet it had an *official* or *regal* appearance. The angel was blowing a long straight trumpet, like the ones they had in the days of the Temple.

The sound of the trumpet was the most striking part of the appearance, other than the sheer size of the angel. It was a low, mournful type of sound that almost sounded far away. It would occasionally crescendo, then dip and almost disappear—but you could always hear the low mournful sound underneath. It is hard to describe. I listened and understood that it was a sound that would resonate within Jewish hearts—and those like mine, who have a circumcised heart for the Lord and the purposes of God regarding His chosen people, the Jews. There was a deep longing in the sound. It was as if the sound of this trumpet was calling hearts that could hear it to this place, Israel, Jerusalem, the Old City, to this very spot near the western wall of the Temple Mount.

Comment: I am not Jewish, and I am not one of those who strongly desire to be. Yet I love God and recognize His special love for His people and His land. One of my favorite questions to ask when people bring up the subject and ask if someone is Jewish or not, is—What's the definition of Jewish? It truly depends on whom you are talking to. Israel has been so scattered for so many years, intermarrying and hiding identities—that there may be a speck of Israeli DNA in much of the world by this time. Those we call Jewish, that the nation of Israel calls Jewish, are only from the tribes of Judah, Benjamin, and maybe a few Levites. The rest of the tribes were completely lost amongst the nations, but the Bible clearly states they are all part of God's plan of restoration in the end time.

I believe there are those like myself that hear the sound, just because of their close relationship with the Father and who understand His Heart and His love for these chosen people who have suffered so much over thousands of years, for His Name's sake. The trumpet call is to the Temple Mount area, in Jerusalem, but more importantly to Him.

It is significant to me that I received this vision in the night the night after I actually went to the Temple Mount for the first time. I have been visiting Israel since March 2002, but the Temple Mount had been closed to all except Muslims. In July 2003, it was reopened. I was connected with a group that was allowed access that September—no praying allowed, but we could silently talk to God.

The other significant event that happened within 24 hours of my visit and this vision was that a dear friend passed away after a long battle with cancer. He had been one of my chief intercessors. I cried out to God about all of his family's suffering and how much they and the body of Christ needed him. The Lord then gave me a vision of my friend Phil, twirling in circles and dancing on the pavement in Temple in Heaven with no more pain—as the Lord said to me, "*I need him here.*"

The Ring

February 2004: prophetic, heaven

I had been in God's presence and received His commendation. I cannot recall what it was about though. I didn't feel any particular sense of pride or accomplishment. It was more of an acknowledgement that I had done the job correctly—faithfully—I believe He called it. I thought it was time to leave, but instead I was told to put forth my hand. I put my hand out and a ring was placed on my finger. Although I am not very good at receiving praise or gifts, I didn't protest because I was suddenly and completely awed by the gemstone.

I looked in amazement at the stone in this ring. It was a large, oval emerald gem a little more than a half an inch long. It was like no emerald I have ever seen or imagined. Inside the stone, it was like there was a fire burning. It was so beautiful that it took my breath away. I was speechless.

Comment: This gemstone so captured my attention that I am not sure which hand, or even on which finger, the ring was placed. The ring itself was a golden color, a very simple setting for the living stone. It almost looked like there were flames flickering inside—a fiery emerald.

What does this kind of dream mean? Well, a ring given in this context usually is a sign of honor and can be a badge of authority. That is the way I understood it as I woke up. I didn't want to open my eyes so that I could continue to focus on the image imprinted in my mind of this wonderful gem. I cannot recall why the ring was given, so I don't know what it was exactly that was being rewarded—maybe the event was more like a commissioning, but I have the sense that I really had received something very special from God. I was taken to Heaven, once again, and sent back with a new enablement. To me, it means a new direction for my life, a new understanding of His purposes and new authority in my spiritual walk and ministry. The emerald, my favorite gemstone, reminds me of the throne of God—the authority, wisdom and perspective of God. The fire reminds me of the Spirit of God, His Presence—alive, actually life itself. With the calling comes also the provision—materially, spiritually equipped, and anointed.

A Tiny Castle &
a Humble Woman

June 2004: *vision, servants*

Once there was a woman who kept a small castle. It was a place where travelers could come, stay, and be refreshed. It had a beautiful garden and a peaceful atmosphere. It was a joyful resting place for weary Ministers of God who came and went bringing blessings and receiving blessings from the servant woman who kept the house. She lived worshipping and serving her Lord, dancing with Him in joyful service, graced to bless others and to receive the favor of her Lord in return. One day a man, who was a prince and a bard, stayed for a while at the castle. The woman prayed for, served, and blessed him as she did for all the servants her Lord sent to her home.

Before he left, he kissed her hand. Her heart lifted for just a moment—wondering if she were ever to have the privilege of meeting a passionate, worthy man to serve alongside. But she is quickly reminded that she could never again be a young princess who could bear children and joyfully walk beside such a man as this bard. The wisdom and experience of a more elderly prophet or shepherd would more likely be the Lord's choosing. The Wisdom and Grace of being a seasoned handmaiden herself brought her back to the abiding Love and Presence of her Lord.

She continues to walk in the Garden with her Lord; awaiting the next guest He will send with His Blessings. She smiles as the flowers bloom and fade, reminded to pray for all those who have crossed her path and the threshold of the castle. Storm clouds come and then pass. Along with the storm, sadness passes as loneliness flees with the fresh wind. She smiles, soaking in the sunshine and dreaming of her Lord's embrace.

Comment: This was actually a vision that came to me while I was awake. I was sitting in my living room, pondering on how much the Lord had blessed me with good friends and provided for all my needs. I sat at my laptop and began typing. This is what came out. I've included it here because it was so much like some dreams I've experienced.

Reunion with my Skinny Friend

May 2004: prophetic

I was with friends visiting a very small church in an unknown place. Though it was small, it had a single section of pews rather than folding chairs. I was seated near the front, four or five rows back. There weren't very many people in the church. Each pew would probably hold about twelve people, yet there were only about eight people in all, scattered among the pews in front of me. The service was about to start, and I wondered why there were so few—maybe it was a really small congregation. I turned around to see if the back of the church was also empty.

As I looked at the smattering of people in the ten or so pews behind me, I suddenly saw an unexpected, very familiar face. I jumped up and made my way to the aisle. My friend also jumped up and began moving toward the aisle. It was then that I had noticed that she looked so very different. She had lost so much weight; she was barely a shadow of her former self. She looked *great*! Vibrant and healthy! We met and embraced in a hug that erased the time we hadn't seen each other. It was the most joyous reunion I have ever witnessed.

We both asked each other at the same time, "What are *you* doing *here*?!" And, "I've missed you so much! You look so good!... How awesome is our God!"

Comment: My dear friend and I expect that this dream will one day come to pass. For a season, we have ministered in the same place, but our paths will soon take different directions. I don't look forward to missing my friend, but I do look forward to seeing her again—so thin, healthy, and less stressed than in her current situation. God is faithful.

This dream also shows me how God gives us visions so that we will pray and see them come to pass. Whenever I am in new places, I always expect to see a familiar face. And I do, either an old or new friend will always be there. God directs our paths to cross each other's just to reassure us He is in control always. Sometimes these are divine encounters, planned by Him strategically. Seeing someone receive healing, be delivered, or find themselves in a better situation increases our faith to believe God and stand with others in prayer.

Silent Voices

September 2004: end times

I was in an area of a town, or a city, that had buildings in ruins. The buildings were all made of stone. They were similar to those you might find in the Middle East, except that the stone was redder. One particular building was missing its roof and top two floors. Only the one and a half story wall gave indication of what used to be a large house or apartment. The people were living in the dirt, huddled close to the walls, which gave little protection.

    I was a visitor. A woman silently took me around to a side where there were more people because the remains of the buildings offered a little more protection. The people were in rags. Even a scrap of material protruding from the rubble was quickly confiscated. I gave them the snack I had in my bag, and they gratefully shared it. It seemed so little for some twenty or thirty people that lived in this area. The man who was apparently in charge led me to an opening that went underground. No one spoke at all the entire time. It seemed as if making a noise could cost you your life.

I descended one level of stairs to a passage, which became a corridor similar to an underground mall. The lights were dim and yellow. It gave a strange hue to the stones and everything that was there. Things were for sale, but they looked old and dingy—the light enhancing their ancient appearance. I walked silently looking for a particular shop. People would rush by, bumping into me. I had the sense that they did it purposely, like pickpockets do. But I had nothing of value in my bag. It seemed more like they wanted to jostle me to get a reaction.

I came to the shop that looked like the right one. There was someone speaking with a man in the doorway, so I pretended to look at some things outside of the next shop. When the person left, I quickly came to the door as the man was shutting it. He didn't want to let me in. I could see in the window the things for sale, very old furniture and some cloth, and that it was a shop that should be open. I pointed at the things for sale and he relented. I looked at some cloth that could be used as a scarf. It was a special sign to the shopkeeper, who looked at the cloth and asked a question (I don't remember the question). A woman appeared and the man watched to see if anyone had seen me enter as the woman led me upstairs.

We entered a room resembling a restaurant, where they could feed people secretly. Apparently, it was a crime to have extra food and to feed needy people. They wanted me to eat, or at least have tea, but I refused. I was there only to check and make sure that they were there and still able to function, but we couldn't speak. Everything was communicated by actions. I hugged them then went downstairs as if I was a casual shopper once again. I left the shop and continued down the corridor.

I traveled a short way until I was out of sight of that shop before I relaxed my gate and acted as if I was shopping again. Children ran by again, acting like pickpockets. I paid them no notice except to hold my bag closer. Then suddenly I was blinded by the glare of a spotlight. It was as if police came, pushed you around a little, and asked who you were and what you were doing, but I couldn't really see anyone. I just knew I was being questioned. I responded with my first name—that was all they found necessary, and told them I was a traveler passing through. They hesitated and then said I must leave immediately. I didn't really know which way to go out but walked the way they indicated. I was hoping and praying that they would not find out about the people I had just left. If their focus stayed on me, it was okay, but I knew it was dangerous to even think of the people, any of the people, I had met. I just tried to concentrate on my footsteps and where the new passageway was leading.

Comment: This is one of those troubling dreams. It seems a picture into end-times, where few are left and even fewer are believers. This was a time of persecution, where believers must live in secret at the price of their lives. It was an intense time of poverty and control by wicked forces. Though I was not in the same dire straights as the people I encountered, it seemed I was absolutely powerless to help. Since I could not speak, my presence was all the encouragement I could give, and, that would come with a high price, if they were caught with me.

Yet the love and compassion that these people showed was as evident as any today. Their faith was evident, without words, without anything really. I woke up admiring and honoring the people I had met. Yet as I go back to my relatively comfortable life I ask, "Lord, let me never forget those desperate faces. Let me never forget those who have no voice, no means to cry out. Let me cry out on their behalf, may my voice continually be lifted up in their stead. Have mercy, Father God, have *mercy*."

Airplane that Flies Straight Up

September 2004: end times, airplane

I was on the tarmac at the Los Angeles International Airport. I've only traveled through LAX once, yet I recognized the surroundings because I instinctively knew where I was. I was about to board a very small jet when I looked up and saw one of the really large planes just overhead. It was at least the size of a Boeing 767. It was strange though because it was flying so close to the terminal and just above our heads. No one seemed to panic though, and there was no crash, so I got on my plane.

We had to wait a really long time. Apparently, there was a backup in planes trying to take off. Some kind of emergency was going on in California and people were leaving. All the flights were full. I was happy just to have been able to get on a plane. It would take off eventually. The view out my window was of the other small planes on the tarmac. They seemed to be leaving from a smaller runway than the big jets. Then I saw the big plane again. It was pushed back a short way from the terminal close to the smaller planes. The engines started, and I saw it lift directly up from the ground like a helicopter would. Then, as if hanging in the air, it lifted the nose to vertical and shot straight up into the air—really fast! I suddenly realized that what I was seeing earlier was the same plane landing. It just kind of stopped in the air, like at a stop sign, and sat down.

My impression was that this was some secret thing that was brought out because of the emergency need to move people out of the area efficiently. Somehow, I felt that the people didn't realize, even while riding on that plane, what it was doing or what was happening. I looked around and no one seemed to be noticing anything unusual out the windows, but I knew I had witnessed something covert.

Comment: Okay, this is another one of those *impossible* dreams. So what does it mean? It is unlikely that such a plane exists, but it may mean that some secret means of evacuating people does exist. It didn't seem like there was any panicked rush of people trying to get away. It seemed efficient and orderly. After what happened with the catastrophe in New Orleans, it is hard to imagine the government doing anything in a disaster *decently and in order*. However, I think the greater message again is: Trust God.

The other message I get, which I have gotten repeatedly when I have dreamed about disastrous things that have happened, is that I am fine, calm, observant and useful. God gives me a vantage point to see a bigger picture. I survive very ominous situations and often help others, too. I don't at all relish the idea of being a survivor and having to deal with devastation. I'd much rather die and be with the Lord, but that is apparently not His plan.

This could also be an illustration of watching a ministry or move of God that seems to do the impossible. Something that should have crashed, is taking off straight up toward heaven to victory. The secretive part would be that the enemy is unaware and cannot figure out what God is doing. Wouldn't it be amazing if the Lord has planned a massive revival for a huge city like LA, where nearly all the city would be caught up in salvation and serving the Lord? So much so, that fear and panic cannot affect a city of millions. Hallelujah!

Five Dollar Bills

December 2004: provision

I was visiting someplace unfamiliar. I went with a couple others—all men—in one of the men's grey sports car. I thought I liked it because it was similar to mine—the man must have had similar taste. They let me sit in the front seat. The driver was average looking—average height though a little thin and short sandy hair—almost wavy with a red tint in the sun. I liked him; we all talked, and I laughed. He had a soothing voice and manner. I remember he took us to see some interesting things.

Once while stopped, I opened the door to get a better view. As I sat in the seat, with one leg out the door, I stretched to put a twenty-dollar bill in the pocket of my jeans. I saw a five-dollar bill on the ground within arm's reach. As I noticed the sandy ground, I remembered this was the fourth five-dollar bill I had found that day. One was in the snow, one now in the sand—*where did I see the other two?*

Then we were in a building, a residence. I sat down feeling exhausted. Next thing I knew I was asleep, then waking, seeing this same man across the room and reaching for him because I didn't want to be alone. Exhausted, I groaned but couldn't move. He didn't notice me. I fell back asleep.

Comment: The number five usually speaks of grace, to me this indicates unmerited favor—or supernatural ability to do something that is beyond my natural ability or capability. Because it is money in this dream, it could be supernatural grace concerning money, or provision—from unusual places. I can't even remember where the money appeared from because the provision just seems to continue.

The car and being in the company of men, seems to me to be a place of familiarity. I have worked in software engineering for over fifteen years and most of my co-workers were men. (Even while growing up, I enjoyed my brother's company—and especially his toys, like cars—more than being with my sisters and their dolls.)

I felt comfortable and content expecting God to provide. Yet at the point, I put the money in my pocket, the situation changed. I had moved on to a new situation. I was in an unfamiliar residence and with a companion who seemed unfamiliar, yet I was very at ease with him. In myself, I was insecure and exhausted. I couldn't express myself. It seemed he either couldn't hear or understand me and then I fell asleep.

I believe the man represented the Holy Spirit. He is The Comforter. He directs us and instructs us, and He never leaves us. Even if I sometime *feel* alone, He is there. Our perspective of God changes as we grow in the knowledge and grace of the Lord. Even in our times of doubt, He never changes. God is faithful.

The Three Doors

December 2004: prophetic

The Lord was speaking with me in my dream about a choice He was offering me. I had to make a decision, and I was kind of looking to Him—not having a clue about how I could decide. In fact, I didn't even know what I was trying to decide about. He very slowly and carefully explained my choices. God speaks to me mostly in pictures, so He was both showing and telling me as He spoke.

He presented the three choices to me like three doors. They were doors that looked quite like the TV show where the grand prize was the person's choice of Door #1, Door #2, or Door #3. The doors looked identical to me, so He explained further.

Door #1 Affluence: Here was my opportunity to have those blessings that were very dear to me. The red Corvette I had always kidded about owning. I didn't really want one all that much, but knew that all things are possible through Christ. I could have it all if I chose this door. There was much more that went with that kind of affluence. A big house so I could open it up for more missionaries and ministers to stay was part of this choice. The ability to go to more countries on missions' trips was behind this door—promotions at work to fill the bank account so I could have more to give away. With the promotions, more doors would open in marketplace ministry to those in upper management that really don't think they need Jesus, people who have material things but whose lives are actually empty like anyone who does not know the Lord. All these were good things, and all would be received in a godly way—living really well and sharing every bit of it with the body of Christ. I gleefully pictured the faces of those I could offer the keys to the Corvette during their stay. This was a blessed choice.

Door #2 Comfort: Here was the opportunity to continue on in the way I had been. My life was good. I had enough and some left over to give away. I had amazing testimonies and great influence in marketplace ministry that would continue to slowly grow as I was a steady witness in my job. My finances would continue to recover from being stolen from in my past. My pension, which had taken a hit with the stock market and job transitions, was stable and beginning to slowly rise. One day I could retire! The American dream—which having lived on public assistance for so long—I never thought I could embrace. I would be in my nice house God had given me, near my grandchildren, and growing in my ministry and responsibility at our church. It appeared to be all good. God was obviously just as pleased with this choice.

Door #3 Challenge: The Lord said, "This is the most difficult choice." He uses few words when He speaks to me, but I knew inside by the way He was presenting this choice that it represented His best option. I was about to answer that His choice was, of course, my choice, when He added, "This will be harder than everything you have ever been through before." Wow, that hit me hard. My mind was flooded remembering when my daughter died, and I almost died. I remembered when my son was minutes from death from a bee sting. Then I remembered my absolute shock and disappointment when my husband walked away from God and back into alcoholism, forcing me to leave him to protect the children. I remembered going back to college and standing scared to death in front of university professors with my knees shaking uncontrollably, desperate to win a scholarship. I thought about the two more tragic divorces I had endured and my two older boys leaving for the Army just before 9/11. As these things flooded my mind, God also poured His grace into my spirit. I looked toward Him with resolve. God had always seen me through—every single experience that could come to my mind—and He wasn't going to change. I confidently said, "I want to do this."

Comment: I woke up exhausted, but satisfied. I knew I would never doubt my decision because the Lord had so carefully walked me through my choices. I didn't know how my life would change, but I knew that as of that day it would. I believe that God purposely doesn't show us details ahead of time because we just can't handle knowing them. I know me; I'd rush into something and mess up God's perfect timing. I was not looking to rush into the difficult unknown. Well, maybe a little, but there was definitely a check in my spirit about the deliberateness of God's orchestration, to bring all this about—whatever "this" was.

Although I had a relative face-to-face conversation with God, I didn't see Him with my eyes. I didn't try to look at Him; this was Father God! You know how to act when you are in His presence—and you just do it. The scripture that says, "That at the name of Jesus every knee should bow, of things in heaven, and things in earth, and things under the earth; And that every tongue should confess that Jesus Christ is Lord, to the glory of God the Father" (Philippians 2:10–11). Well, it isn't because they have a choice—your body just does what it's supposed to do in God's Presence.

The other thing about this dream was I realized that it really was okay, for me to make any of the three choices. When God gives us choices, He blesses our choices. I know some people go around fretting that if they choose this or that they may miss God's perfect will. I see God as taking even my bad choices that He didn't even offer and working them for my good and His glory as I submit my life to Him with each footstep. Sometimes the world screams at us so loudly that it is very difficult to decide what might be God's best choice for us. That's what grace is all about. You realize you messed up, repent, and walk toward God again. Willful disobedience can kill you though. When God gives you a choice, seek His will then make the choice. Don't waste your time sitting on a fence. He is faithful to guide us and is faithful to save us, even picking us up when we fall in our weakness. He *is* forever faithful.

Airplane Crash

December 2004: *airplane, end times*

I was walking beside a road along an open field. The road was narrow but paved. The fields were a golden color of tall grass swaying gently in the wind. It was peaceful. Suddenly I heard a tremendous roar coming toward me. It was so loud I couldn't quite tell which direction it was coming from. I instinctively ducked, feeling the sound must be coming from above me. There were no trees or ditches where I could take cover. A short distance ahead of me was a building. I watched in astonishment as a huge airplane, at least as big as a Boeing 717, came perpendicular to the road, just above the ground barely missing the building. It was flying too fast to crash land, yet at the angle it approached; I knew it would crash. I held my breath and closed my eyes as I dove down on the ground waiting for the explosion.

There was no explosion. The ground rumbled as the nose of the airplane literally impaled the ground and the plane came to a stop. People rushed out of the building where some of the windows broke with the tremors. But I told them to stay back. I was certain that the plane would blow up any minute, with the fuel and hot engines touching the ground.

The back door near the tail of the plane opened and people began to evacuate the airplane. I was amazed that so many people had survived and were apparently unharmed. They jumped down and stared at the plane. I grabbed them and pointed them toward the building to seek shelter underground because of the pending explosion. I began to think that God had a purpose for their survival, that there must be someone on that plane that was not supposed to die because it was all so impossible. What I was seeing with my eyes was impossible! God allowed this to happen literally at my feet, so that I could calmly point the people to safety. I didn't have any more time to think, as the last of the people came out of the plane. I knew we had seconds to get away. We all ran toward the building, falling on the pavement as the explosion rocked the place and debris began to rain on us.

Comment: I don't understand all the symbolism in this dream, but I do understand that our footsteps are directed by the Lord. The more we cooperate with him, the more precise those steps can be. The Lord has handcrafted us, our personalities as well as our bodies. He knows the experiences we live, even from before we are saved, shape our reactions. God was confirming to me that He has given me this gift of being calm and logical in panicky situations. He has given me wisdom (that I am often not aware of) that He can use to bless others while He receives all the glory. Impossible things can and do happen. We all need to be prepared to listen to the still small voice of God, whether it is thundering or quiet! Lives may be at stake, including our own.

A friend has offered some insight to the symbolism in this dream. I have prayed about it and feel this is probably what the Lord was speaking to me. The plane crash represents a "doctrinal crash" in some people's theology. Those who survived escaped through the tail, which can be a symbol of false teaching or false prophecy. My surprise that so many had survived is significant, and my being able to instruct and direct them to safety *just in time* is also significant. The golden fields speak of the harvest that has not enough laborers. Immediately when this person suggested these things one thing burst forth in my mind: I have been very concerned for my brothers and sisters in the Lord about what I call the *escapism theory* of the commonly taught information about the *rapture*. I don't want to get into the entire discussion here, but it is a passionate burden of my heart to get out the truth about trusting God, so that people won't perish or fall away in their disappointment when the false expectations of avoiding tribulations do not materialize.

Six months after this dream, I suddenly entered full-time ministry. I hope to, in some small way, make a difference in both of these areas—the harvest of lost souls and encouraging believers to trust the Lord *through* every trial and difficulty.

On Her Face
with God

March 2005: vision of God

This is a waking vision. It was quite unusual, as I was driving to work on a snowy day on the freeway—in the passing lane. I was singing along with a Jason Upton worship song about meeting Jesus face to face, when I suddenly saw this vision—while driving sixty miles per hour. It was 8:35 a.m. I still feel the impact of the vision. Tears fill my eyes even as I write this.

I saw a woman I know, Laura, on her knees on a carpet in the middle of a room. It appeared to be in a home setting, like a living room. She had her head bowed low. While she was sitting back on her feet, her arms were outstretched. She was interceding. Her mouth was moving and in earnest as she bent low toward the ground. Her face almost touched her knees as her hands lay on the floor palms up in front of her.

As I looked at her, I sensed her prayer was one of deep admiration and love for the Lord. She was calling out to see His face, wanting more of Him. I then saw the Lord just two feet away from her. He was bent toward her, with such a loving expression on His face, listening closely, to hear each word—even the unspoken ones. I cried out, "Lord if she would just look up, she *would* see You. You are so close!" I was sobbing. I felt so privileged to have been given this quick glimpse into a relationship so intimate and at such moving moment.

Comment: It was difficult to compose myself to continue driving to work. Later the Lord showed me just how limited my own sight was. You see, Laura didn't need to raise her eyes to look into the face of God. With her eyes tightly shut and her head bowed low, *she was looking directly into his face.* This picture of true worship will forever be burned into my memory.

Living in the Supernatural

Matter
Transforming

August 2006: prophetic

I stepped out of a stone building onto the sidewalk. I turned and noticed that the building directly next door was partially torn down, with some of the rubble beginning to spill onto the sidewalk. (The place reminded me of many such places in Jerusalem) One of my friends was on top of the pile trying to clear out some of the dirt that kept falling onto the sidewalk. The site was a narrow place (approximately fourteen feet wide) between two stone houses. We were gathered in the house on the right of the seemingly broken down house. There were about six or eight young adults (in their twenties or thirties) going in and out of the house trying to clean up the sidewalk where dirt and rocks kept falling, while one worked on a project at the top of the pile.

This one, apparently an archaeologist, called to everyone to come and look at what he had uncovered and had been working on while we were busy. It was an old model of an ancient place of worship, mostly covered with caked dirt.

When someone's shovel hit the ground, the dirt started falling off and portions of the brown color of the model turned into black as it was transformed into another elaborate model of a different place of worship. Suddenly, I was awed by the black delicate ribbons of carbon that stood impossibly on edge near the border of the model. They couldn't have survived the caked dirt; one's breath could move them.

Then the entire board transformed before my eyes. A number of different models of places of worship appeared one after another as the matter transformed. It seemed these models came from different times and cultures, but the scenes were brief and then more molten transformations took place. Finally, a beautiful gem appeared that was azure, turquoise, and white. The most beautiful blue gem I could ever have imagined. The molten gem was morphed into shape near the center of yet another place of worship. Its shape was of a sort of dragon-like figure carved on the face of the five-inch diameter gem housed in a black ornate metal. It had soft features though, so I thought that *it* must have been the original that has since transformed into the typical Asian dragon that is used so often to embellish a piece of art in Japan. This was a dragon that had no demonic connotations or grotesqueness. It was as beautiful as the gem.

Then both the gem and its container flowed to the side of the *picture*. What took up the rest of the scene was a black enameled table and chair set with beautiful artistry. They appeared metal, yet didn't have that cold feel—appearing more like wood. As I touched them, I realized they were now life size furniture. There were ivy and other artistic embellishments that looked like they were literally alive, full of color and vibrancy. They were a blue-green-silver. It was a beautiful masterpiece unlike anything I had ever seen before and indescribable by human words. I felt overwhelming beauty as I gazed at the scene. Then, as I awoke, I heard myself say the words, "Man has absolutely no concept of the creative imagination that is contained in our brains, even now in our flesh. We were created in the image of God. He has given us undiscovered creative imaginations."

Comment: At the end of the dream, I may have been transported into the model so that it became life size and I was in the midst of it. The black furnishings were those inside the model, but they were like real chairs and tables to me. I was so overwhelmed by the beauty—it filled the room, and I could for the first time touch it. There was only a rope barrier as in a museum.

I have been to places like the mountains in Colorado, the Grand Canyon, and the Highlands in Scotland—places that are so beautiful that it takes your breath away. The wonder and beauty of a newborn baby or the birth of a super-nova in space are things that are magnificent and fill our senses, but the beauty I sensed in these pieces at the end of this dream is something I have never comprehended before. I can't begin to explain it. It was kind of like something beyond our five senses.

The dream had great meaning for a friend who was about to embark on a ministry trip to Japan. We have other friends that are connected there, but I have never had any special draw to anything Japanese. To me, the idea of matter having the ability to *morph* into other matter is a compelling thought, sounding more like science fiction. However, in the dream it was a means of teaching and showing how things change over periods of time in how man perceives worship and honoring God. The places of worship flowing from the natural stones, like the altars built in Abraham's day, to the Tabernacle of Moses' day, to the Temple of Solomon's day would be a similar concept in my understanding. The end of the dream, though black and reminding me of Japan after I awoke, was more like looking into a future where all matter is transformed. We will have resurrected bodies. I guess that means walking through walls isn't a problem because that's what Jesus did in the book of Acts. We are to experience a new heaven and a new earth; the sky will be rolled up as a scroll. All these things are beyond our comprehension—and certainly, matter transforming before our eyes is as well.

The Lord has since shown me that the different models actually represent *mindsets*. As we grow spiritually, we gain more and more of the Lord's perspective, and we are able to operate more in the supernatural. This dream seems to be a picture of my heart for the Lord, my spiritual growth. The very first model was so basic, even the delicate carbon ribbon represented my fragile new faith and understanding of God. The earthy mud was my earthy nature, newly reborn. The other models were not of great remembrance, simply progression toward the present, until the final model. It became life size. This indicates to me that I am able to step into my destiny and operating in the supernatural. The beauty was breathtaking. The revelation of God's purpose, shown by the dragon, which the enemy had corrupted for years, is within our grasp. I was awed and hesitant to step into the model. The simple rope barriers represented access through proper protocols and not presumption. The revelation of what is available to me, to all of us serving the Lord wholeheartedly, is staggering.

I am blessed, as I realize the model was always a place of worship. God has been pleased to receive my worship, even in its crude state in the first model—it was beautiful. The words that came as I woke up challenge me to consider that God wants us to expand even our imaginations. We need to gain His perspective and use our words to call things that are not, as though were—as in 1 Corinthians 1:28. But it is even more than that. *Lord, give us your thoughts, your ideas—breakthrough our simplistic modes of thinking to release the secrets you long to share with us!*

Serving

November 2006: servants, prophetic, provision

I found myself in a kitchen with a few people. I was busily preparing refreshments for a women's gathering in the next room. It was a fairly large kitchen, yet it still seemed like it was a home, not a facility. I was volunteering to fill in—apparently, no one had planned this ahead of time. I scurried around and guided everyone into the next room. Before leaving, someone helped me find cups for tea or coffee. There were only very tiny plastic cups the size of demitasse cups. Surprisingly, they said that they would be perfect. I put them out on the table with a strange coffee dispenser. It was an oblong teapot-like thing, which had a coffee spout on one side and a waterspout on the other. Very strange—yet it seemed to work, so I put it out on the table in the next room for the guests.

Then I set to work checking the oven. When I opened the door there were lots of huge breaded fish fries. They were in two pans, and they were falling all over the inside of the oven, sliding off the pans because there were so many.

It wasn't time yet to put them on the table. I recall exclaiming to myself, "They are perfectly baked!" Very large and perfectly browned, everyone would be very pleased. I shut the oven door hoping the delay in serving would turn out okay—they were so perfectly cooked right now. I trusted that they would still be perfect, even though they were kind of spilling over in abundance. I sat down for just a moment at the table with my back to the room. I picked up a piece of the cracker like bread and dipped it in a small dish of sauce sitting in front of me. Suddenly, I realized the people in the next needed to be served the fish, and I shouldn't be resting and enjoying myself.

Someone was watching me through the door, and I felt guilty for sitting and tasting. I quickly jumped up, still chewing, to serve everything and wondering if there had been enough cups and coffee. I was thinking I wasn't a very good server. I knew there were a lot of people in the next room—mostly women but some men. But, since no one had come to get anything, it must be okay. Then I awoke.

Comment: It strikes me that I didn't really have to prepare anything. The coffee was made and already in the serving pot. The fish were already cooked and the sauce and cracker bread were just there—waiting to be served. I volunteered to serve, even though I didn't know what I was really volunteering to do. I didn't realize there was food, only drinks, when I volunteered. I have just read that fish can indicate grace. It makes sense to me that Jesus always multiplied loaves and fishes (Matthew 14, Mark 6, Luke 9, and John 6). The bread almost seems like it was matzo. To me, bread relates to the bread of life—Jesus, the Word made flesh.

I think the interpretation is something like: God has given me an assignment to serve His provision to others. He will prepare it, provide it, and multiply it as necessary—even providing the place (The ministry we have now does this on a small scale). But that fish was so perfect and so abundant! I believe He is going to increase the amounts to overflowing for everything we give out in ministry—both spiritual and natural food, as provision. Praise God!

Train Stations

November 2006: prophetic

I was on a modern train with a small amount of luggage and headed for an airport. The train was apparently a metro-rail of sorts but in a country setting. I first viewed the landscape and began to search for the train station as the train crested a hill. Straight ahead was a station, but there were no signs or layout indicating the airport was at that stop. I could also see another train station a little ways to the left before the tracks bent further left almost back toward where we had come from. I decided that it might be the correct stop, and if not, I would get right back on the train for the next stop. I was thinking I still had some time before I had to board the plane at 10:30 a.m.

After exiting the train, I looked around. The station looked a lot like a mall, with shops and small restaurants but so do some airports. Curious, I strolled around the place. I must have been in a foreign place. I didn't seem to be able to communicate with people, and there either weren't signs or I couldn't read them. There were some interesting things, which caught my attention, and I suddenly realized that too much time had passed. As I ran to get back on the train because it was 10:10 a.m., I decided I should check my ticket to see if I could possibly make the 10:30 a.m. flight. I didn't recall the boarding time. When I stopped and dug out the ticket from my luggage, all I could read in the upper right corner was 10:00. *Oh, no!* It was already too late. How could I have made such a mistake? I would have to spend the night.

Suddenly, it was the next morning. I had stayed in a room with two other ladies who were acquaintances, but not really friends. I was helping them get their luggage to the train and warning them about the difficulty in finding the correct stop. They had to catch the next train or they wouldn't be able to make the flight, which left at 10:00 a.m., not 10:30 a.m. They had too much *stuff,* and they were very difficult to get going. We went back and forth to the room and, conveniently, the door didn't lock between trips so it was quicker to get their luggage out. So, they were there waiting, ready before the train came. I ran back to the room and tried to close my last suitcase to run back out the door after them.

When I looked around the room, I saw things in corners, under the bed, the closet, and bathroom that they had left. I ran around the room gathering their remaining things and found an extra empty suitcase to put it all in. One last look and I found some things of mine I had also forgotten. *Thank you, Lord, it was worth it so I wouldn't have to ever come back to this place to get these important things.* Stuffing the last things into the outer zipper pocket, I looked at my watch. 10:00 a.m. I had missed the plane again!

I slowly walked out of the room, wondering this time if

the door would lock and if my ticket would still be good. I had missed two flights, why would they honor my ticket? And, I still wasn't sure I knew the correct exit from the train. Regardless, I decided I would get on that train, find the airport, and stay there until I actually got on the plane.

Comment: I don't really understand fully the significance of the times. The number ten usually indicates divine law or divine economy, as in the Ten Commandments, and the tithe. Because all the tens are associated with time, I believe it has to do with God's divine timing. Part of me is grieved that I was unprepared and missed that timing in the dream, but I was determined to help others and not allow it to happen again—so to fix my mistake. It may have been that the *divine timing* was to miss the plane, yet continue in those footsteps laid out by the Lord letting *Him* guide.

I am familiar with the frustrations of traveling and traveling with others. Not understanding which train station was the correct one reminds me of the difficulties in finding the ministries that God would have you involved in. Here in Israel, there is so much need. You can be pulled in many directions, thereby becoming completely consumed and perhaps missing the ministry that God has called you to. He is gracious, and if we wake up from our distractions and seek Him, He promises to guide us. He will even point us back in the right direction when we get off course.

I see myself as being instrumental to instruct others even when I am still on the journey myself. This is very much like the ministry God has given me over the years, but there is a warning, in that I should be careful not to miss the opportunities God has for me, even when I am doing something worthy for others. God's perfect timing is not set in stone. If we seem to miss an opportunity, yet continue to seek His will and trust Him to work everything for His glory and our good, He can redeem any situation. It could be that the entire mission I was on, was to direct those ladies and be a blessing to them—not to arrive at a particular destination myself. We must remain open and flexible to be, to go and to do whatever He asks of us.

Perhaps this dream is showing me that God has more for us than we are currently involved in. I believe this is true and this dream is a confirmation. We have received invitations to many nations. Until the Lord directs us clearly, and we have the finances, *the ticket*, to go, we cannot get too settled in our current situation. We must be alert to His divine timing and expect His divine resources to be our provision. *Yes, God! Hineni! Here I am!*

Armies & Horses

November 2006: prophetic, spiritual warfare

I saw an army marching on a dirt road through a wooded area. There was another similar regiment that had gone in another direction, off to my left. Each troop continued for as far as I could see. Oddly, the regiment in front of me had covered themselves with a single, huge tarp like camouflage, about fourteen feet wide. This prevented me from viewing the soldiers themselves. I was straining to see if there was a break in the tarp far up ahead, when suddenly they all simultaneously began running to their right. They continued to run through the trees, holding this tarp above their heads while charging. I was at an observation point where I thought, *"This is impossible."* There were no breaks in the tarp, and there are trees that they are running between. Strange.

As my vantage point changed, I saw them become a mass of soldiers leaving the edge of the woods and running into a large open field. It was like a giant meadow. Suddenly the mass of people became a herd of cows stampeding! There were thousands of them. They ran left and right, swerving as though driven madly. I found myself as a cow as well, standing at the end of the field where I sensed they would have to run to continue. I began thinking that I couldn't possibly begin running fast enough to not get completely trampled and killed. As they were weaving back and forth heading in my direction, I chose an estimated perpendicular path to them so that I could quickly get to the edge of their group and perhaps avoid getting trampled. In that split second, I began running as fast as my cow legs would carry me.

My plan worked. The thousands of cows moved past, back in the same direction the army had originally come from, only now they traversed the rough meadow, not on the road. As they ran past, I noticed a few stray cows on the edge of the herd that just slowly stopped running. There were a couple cows in every direction, around the meadow. As they slowed, I suddenly observed a wolf run stealthily in from a wooded area to the right, skirting the woods straight ahead to attack the weary animals as they came to rest. At the same time, the cows changed into horses. I did as well. They realized the wolf was after them, and they would run in arcs around each other. The wolf would chase one horse, then switch to another as it came within his reach—all the time getting closer and closer to successfully attacking. As one horse came wildly rushing toward me, I realized either the wolf thought he could get him, or he would be on my tail in a moment. Either way, it was a bad situation.

As the wolf approached, I decided to act like a horse and, instead of running, I rose up on my hind legs and began thrashing my front legs wildly. I was attempting to attack the unsuspecting wolf. It was strange because I saw my front legs as hands, as if I was human. In a flash I thought, *This has to look pretty silly. Yet, I'm supposed to be a horse so I'm going to act like one.* It worked and the wolf was vanquished. The six or eight of us then began to gather and walk slowly back toward the road. As we came together, we became humans again. One young man had a bad gash on his face. Apparently, the wolf had gotten very close to getting him. He took no notice of it, as any brave young soldier would act. They were simply chatting, joking, and heading back toward the road to continue the journey.

Comment: Cows often represent false teaching or false prophets. In the context of this dream it would seem that men that were supposed to be an Army (God's Army), ran from under the tarp (God's sovereign protection), gradually losing their covering as they ran through the woods. The woods can represent human doctrine that opposes the work and word of the Holy Spirit. They became cows that were stampeding in a different direction, the opposite direction that they were originally headed. I had not run through the woods; I had been observing from above it. I had identified myself with them, but I was not in a position to help much except to save myself from their unintentional danger to me.

Those few, who had perhaps identified with them as I did or were temporarily deluded, were the cows who were left—a remnant. They became horses. Horses can be a symbol of a supernatural warrior. These were the true warriors from the Army of God. Immediately the wolf—the enemy, Satan—appeared to attack the warriors. They ran, not understanding the power that had been given them to fight. Only in the desperation of imminent defeat, I stepped forward to fight as the warrior of God. When the victory came, we became the Army again and walk back to the road, back onto the intended path.

God used the enemy's plans to purge the Army, to train, and to raise up the true warriors. After joining their battle, I became part of their ranks. Again, this dream reminds me of the deception of the pre-tribulation rapture which teaches that the church will not go through great tribulations. Saints, some of us already are going through it.[12]

After experiencing this dream, I got out the Bible and found that this dream reminds me of Joel 2. I do know that whatever battles face us, now or in the last days, the Lord has promised to equip us. He is our shield, our high tower of refuge, our strength, our guide, our rear-guard and so much more! Trusting in His love and grace for every situation will enable us to win every battle. No weapon formed against us can prosper (Isaiah 54).

Your Need His Provision

November 2006: prophetic, provision

In this dream, I was standing with another person when someone fell at my feet in agony. This person was very, very ill. She was dressed in filthy rags. I understood, as she reached her contorted hand toward me, that the doctors had been unable to help her. She could only half crawl, half walk and fell in agony every few steps. I was overwhelmed with pain for her. I am not a person overly compassionate or possessing the gift of mercy, so my emotions were not the part of me that responded. I felt, or thought, that there must be something that could be done for her. I stretched out my right hand toward her and said one word. I didn't know what the word was, but I thought it might be Hebrew, malay. The woman let her head fall and sighed. She had been healed. She didn't get up or even move, but her sigh indicated that she had received what she needed.

I didn't stay to see if she would get up, or if she could. It didn't seem important. I looked around and saw others, not far away, in similar condition—desperately ill and in rags. I thought, "If it worked once—try it again." There were both men and women, dressed very much alike. The one word spoken seemed to work, as one after another sighed, or collapsed—but always in relief, having received. I wandered among them, with the person beside me observing.

Comment: I have several times received prophecy that I have healing hands. Some have anointed my hands with oil as a symbol of this. I have never gone around healing people—like Benny Hinn—but I have had occasions of praying and seeing miracles. Three years ago, I had an experience during communion at the Garden Tomb in Jerusalem, where a tiny wooden communion cup was leaking on my hand while the leader was being a little long winded. I was trying to pay attention, but kept thinking that I would miss taking the wine (grape juice) because of this problem. Suddenly the Lord spoke gently to my heart, "This time *I* am anointing your hands."

I began crying and almost spilled the rest of the juice. There was a big enough drop left for communion, and my hand was all wet and sticky. For the first time in my life, I really felt like the juice was the blood of Jesus to anoint, cleanse, and prepare my hands for service. We have seen more miracles since traveling to Uganda where people are healed of AIDS and major diseases. I have yet to see a real fulfillment of this level of anointing. This dream reminds me of these words.

I shared with a friend who thought this dream was a picture of the end times. Since we live in Israel, there is always the threat of war and terrible bombings (People don't realize we all have bomb shelters here—and gas masks. Terror is a reality we live with—but those of us who know Jesus as Messiah should have no fear). My friend could be right about the end times. The people looked as though they might be survivors of something awful.

I still felt like there was more to the meaning. The word really didn't seem all that important. It wasn't like a magic word—a cure-all. It was more like the Lord put a word in my mouth that was perfect for that situation. I didn't know the situation or the cause, and I wasn't sure I had faith to pray and see any results. It was purely a spontaneous leading.

As I was hanging clothes outside, I heard the Israeli children playing in the park, and they said a word that sounded similar though a bunch of Israeli four-year-olds are hard to understand. Maybe that is a confirmation that it was a *God Word*. The Hebrew word mahleh (pronounced ma-lay') means full. Perhaps I was saying, "Be filled."

It is likely the view I saw of the people represented their spiritual condition. Like the Bible describes man as *poor, wretched, blind, diseased with sin, unregenerate*. Even those who are saved—have trusted in the Lord Jesus and His Blood—do not walk in 100% wholeness. We work out our salvation, toward becoming like Him, as a gradual process. When we first accept the Lord, He comes in and begins doing house cleaning, but we have to cooperate or our progress is very slow. It takes our entire lifetime to become all He intends us to be.

These people were full of suffering. God replaced the suffering in them with the Spirit of God. Their relief probably came as they sensed the end of their suffering (There is a suffering in man that may have nothing to do with his physical health). This interpretation of the dream seems most likely to me. Physical healing can follow, or the Lord may take you home in peace. Either way it brings that kind of sigh of relief.

My companion in the dream was most definitely a symbol of the Holy Spirit being with me, guiding my words, my hands, my steps, even my thoughts. God's Word says that if we commit our ways unto Him our thoughts will be established (Proverbs 16:3). That indicates that we will begin to see from His perspective, be motivated by His love, and expect the impossible. In every situation, His grace will forever be sufficient!

Red Carpets

December 2006: prophetic, houses

This dream centers on the purchase of a house. I found myself in a discussion with a lawyer about the price at what appeared to be a pre-closing meeting. I was agreeing to the final price of $129,000. I thought this seemed the right price, as it was the same as the last house I recently sold. I partially expressed this out loud. Strangely, the thought of how much the house might be worth, never entered my mind. I finished the conversation as my mind wandered off thinking—that wasn't really the price I had sold the other house for... but with closing costs and lawyer fees—it would probably calculate quite closely. But why had I stated it this way?

I was then concentrating on the survey map of the property, a map that combined both the buildings and streets around it and a layout of the rooms of the house to scale. I noted that the house was in a prime location—at the very end of a cul-de-sac. There were only three houses on that side of the street with a nice fence at the edge of the neighborhood. It separated it from the main road in the back and some large building complex to the right. The house appeared to have two stories, but was large enough to be lived in comfortably using only one story (I recall thinking that, but I don't know what it really meant). I thought, *Perfect*!

We were allowed to sleep in the new house overnight, prior to the final sale. The house was completely furnished and everything was almost new, including the carpets, which caught my attention. When deciding where to sleep in our new home, the two children (a young boy and his younger sister) gleefully chose the master bedroom. It had a huge king sized bed and was spacious and carpeted wall to wall. The walls were not square as houses in America, but had a slanted wall (which is done frequently in Israel). The carpet was a regal color red, very dark with large paisley shaped feathery designs. It reminded me of an upscale hotel. The hallway carpet was an even darker, solid color red that coordinated with the bedroom carpet. The sparse furniture was a very light colored, fine-grained wood.

I next found myself in the large building complex next door, heading upstairs on an elevator. I ran into some former co-workers and commented to them that we were just purchasing a house very close by—number 129. I got off on the sixth floor and was walking with someone to show them where the place was. It was as if the house had become an apartment within the building complex. We walked passed a hallway row of apartments, but they were the wrong ones. *Not* 2–129, *just* 129. We then came to the correct apartment. I had to reach into my purse for the key to open the apartment. Then I woke up.

Comment: There are a few strange things about this dream. The number 129 is both the price and house number. The number doesn't have particular meaning to me. One is the number of wholeness and unity. Two is the number of covenant, as in marriage or partnership. Nine is the number of gestation or matured development. If you add them together, it is twelve. Twelve is the number of men holding spiritual power and government in their hands.

As I review these possible meanings, I am reminded that in the ministry my husband and I have we are very much in unity. The Lord has brought both of us individually to a place of maturity and joined us in the covenant of marriage to serve Him as one. There has been recurring nine-month periods marking our relationship and ministry as God has birthed these things. Twelve is a revelation because not only does it add up to that, but when I look at it I see 12 and 9. It seems part of God's purpose in bringing us together is to place on our shoulders greatly increased authority in spiritual power and government.

The house was both a house and an apartment, both one story and two. There were apparently two apartments that had almost the same house number. I see the house as our ministry. We are flexible, where we live and where we minister. We serve in diverse areas of practical and spiritual counseling and move in healing and the prophetic at times.

Lastly, the two children were mine, but in the natural, my daughter is older than my three sons. My children are all grown, yet this was not a past, but future dream, so they must be symbolic as well. The children speak to me of the nations and the ministries the Lord has us involved in and of the fruitfulness that He intends. They were joyous for the occasion and excited to sleep in the master bedroom. This looks forward to the ultimate joy and success of the ventures the Lord has placed on our horizon and our access to the Father. My joy at seeing them so happy must signify a deep satisfaction with sharing the fruit of our labors.

I see us as symbolically living in the perfect house, in the perfect location, with the perfect size as a happy, healthy family. We are blessed, even if we see none of these in the natural. The situation is a blessing even to co-workers, both secular and co-laborers in the Kingdom of God, who were glad to see me and happy that we would be living nearby.

The red carpets speak to me both of affluence and royalty, but I am also reminded that it is the Blood of Jesus, which I usually associate red with. All the success symbolized in this dream is due only to the grace and mercy of God, who delights in directing our footsteps on His paths.

Worshipping in the Spirit

December 2006: prophetic

I was in a large church during a service. I was seated close to the front, near a wall on the left side facing forward. There was someone speaking, but I couldn't tell who it was or what they were saying. Then the music started. I closed my eyes and soaked in the sound. I had never heard the words or the music before. In fact, I'm not sure there really were words. I thought, *What is this music?* It touched the soul and was the most beautiful melody, and harmony. It almost sounded like a symphony, but I saw only a few musicians when I came in. I was captivated by this beautiful sound. It drew my soul and spirit into adoration of God. It was as if I was participating, singing or playing an instrument, but I had no words and no instrument.

My curiosity overcame my feelings, and I opened my eyes for a moment. Everyone in the place seemed to be in the same state—enjoying and somehow joining in with the music. I looked all the way to the right where some musicians were sitting. There was a pianist and a couple of others. The melody was so intriguing that I studied them more closely. Way over on the other side of that large auditorium was my friend, Laura, sitting at the piano. Her eyes were closed, and she was enraptured with the music—swaying with it's beauty, but it was a very strange sight because she was holding her hands flat and perfectly still, about 2 feet above the piano keys.

The music was not coming from the piano at all, though it was the main instrument in that small worship team. I leaned to an unknown person behind me and whispered, "Look, look at the person playing the piano!" I wanted someone in the room besides me, and Laura, to realize that the music was heaven produced—without any aid of man.

Comment: I don't even know if Laura knows how to play piano. This dream speaks to me of the day that we will truly worship in spirit and in truth, in corporate settings. I enjoy good worship and love music, so I prefer places where the music is of high quality. However, I have been in small places, even homes, where the worship is so *real* that it transcends high quality music. At our church in Uganda, we have only African drums. I am reminded how a small child singing "Jesus loves me this I know for the Bible tells me so" can inspire me as much as Handel's Messiah at times.

May we all come to the place where we are not performing for ourselves or others. Rather, we are just coming together to join our hearts in admiration of our glorious King. I believe we will more and more find our worship joins with the angels who are continually worshipping Him for who He is. When heaven and earth touch in the embracing of our Lord, glory bursts forth in all directions—Light and Life fill our hearts and lives in a way that will never allow us to worship in the same way again.

My House Trailer

December 2006: houses

The dream begins with me going from house to house, peering in through the front door to view the beautiful new homes that my friends and acquaintances had just received. They didn't all look the same, but they were similar. I recall seeing at least three different places. They were all new, nice, and fully furnished. They were on small but nice lots.

There was, however, one odd thing about them. One feature was the same at each house. Each house had a large, beautiful kitchen. They were done with the best tiles, granite countertops, and beautifully designed in different coordinated colors. They had all the amenities and all the utensils—everything one could want in a kitchen. But each kitchen was sunken by several feet from the rest of the house. They were all one-story houses, but you had to look down into the kitchens. I wondered what purpose that could serve, and I wasn't sure I would like this kind of house.

Then I was told we were going to my new house. We went around a corner, and it appeared to be an area of mobile homes.

Not the nice doublewide, prefabricated homes that are popular in some areas of the United States, but the old type—on wheels. I thought, *Well perhaps they will be nice inside…*

I entered a side door, peering in curiously, half expecting disappointment, half expecting a beautiful surprise. In the back of my mind, I was remembering many dreams I have had where the houses just seemed to grow as I went from room to room. Some became beautiful mansions inside—or mazes to try to find your way out of. I was thinking these things even while I was dreaming. I stepped inside the house and had the distinct feeling that it was exactly what I expected. The kitchen wasn't sunken like the other houses, and this was very different from those houses in many wonderful ways. Then I awoke.

Comment: I don't know what I did expect to see. I truly was torn between great blessing and disappointment. I knew I would be satisfied either way, so I guess it didn't matter. The thing that catches my attention is that I was prepared to be either disappointed or pleased about receiving a trailer on wheels. From the outside, it sure didn't appear a nice place to live, but it was given, and I knew I would be happy to receive it though I wished I hadn't seen the "nicer" looking houses first.

I am sure that the wheels spoke of our mobility in the Kingdom of God. Our roots are in Him, not any physical place. The kitchen is the central place where life revolves. It is where I as the homemaker/mom/hostess spent the most time. It is the place where I feel a need to manage, to create order, and to maintain a healthy lifestyle. My perception of contentment with our surroundings has a lot to do with the condition of the kitchen.

I have always been thankful when God has provided even the most meager accommodations for us. I see the best qualities of the place, and I work at cleaning and creatively turning it into *home* very quickly. It is a gift the Lord has given me, which I have had to exercise quite often in the past thirty years or more. We once owned one of these older trailers. I took our three children and our possessions to a friend's house just two days before a tractor-trailer came, hooked up to it, and hauled it away. The bank had repossessed it. A year later, we lived in a small travel trailer. We had to abandon it, and to this day, I don't know what became of it. Therefore, the idea of being given a trailer on wheels has deeper meaning to me as truly temporary accommodations.

Perhaps God is restoring that which was been stolen by the enemy of our souls. Satan steals not only our possessions, but also our peace, hope, and joy—even our expectations of God's blessings. God's love restores those things that count most.

It would seem that even with a nice new house, I focus on the imperfection (like a sunken kitchen) rather than all the nice amenities. When given something less than new and nice, however, I look for the nice and immediately *see* it improved and work toward bringing it to pass.

It's like that with people too. If you see someone who seems to be blessed and has their life together, their imperfections are exposed as you get to know them better. Yet when you encounter someone who has multiple problems and you begin to get to know them, you begin to see the qualities in that person and as you encourage them, those things come most into focus—for both them and you.

God doesn't see anyone as *having it all together*. When He looks at us, He sees our giftings and potential, beyond our brokenness and weakness. Those things are no problem for Him. The Bible tells us He sees us as a finished work, with all the potential to become what He intends us to be. We are His workmanship (Ephesians 2:10). Father God will mold us and make us and continue to work on us until we become all He intends. The better we cooperate with Him, the more blessed we perceive ourselves.

Fulfilling my Destiny

The Journey

December 2006: houses, prophetic

This dream begins with the final portion of an accent to the top of a very high, steep hill. My husband and I were looking up to plan the best path to finally make it to the top. We were a bit tired but both surprised at the amount of energy we still felt after such a rigorous climb. It appeared the best path was straight ahead, but someone owned the property. There was a pretty white picket fence with a gate just ahead.

The place looked friendly. There were brightly colored flowers along the fence and part way up the path toward what must be someone's house. We stopped at the gate to decide if we should go through and around the side of the house when an elderly, very friendly couple appeared welcoming us. They insisted we go right through their house. They would provide whatever refreshment we might require. They were really nice, the kind of people that make you feel at home and truly welcomed, even if you have never met them before. Such a gift of hospitality always comes from God!

As we exited their home fully refreshed, we were surprised to find ourselves already at the very top of the hill, but instead of a huge plateau, there was a drop-off. You couldn't tell how steep the cliff would have been or how high we were because someone had built elaborate staircases. These staircases wound around in every direction. They were beautiful to look at, well made, and obviously perfectly safe for the otherwise treacherous decent. I looked down in awe, as if gazing across a landscape of created beauty.

Each staircase was made exactly the same way, of the same materials—wood tied together. The steps themselves were carefully placed at regular, easy intervals. The sides of the stairs had vertical poles of wood about four inches in diameter tied together closely forming a secure wall on either side of the three-foot wide stairs. The stairs were so beautiful they were inviting. *Which staircase should we choose?* I looked around and saw some tall pine-like trees clumped together at intervals between the stairs. They were so tall that with the winding stairways going in all directions, you couldn't see where they came up from the ground. The strange thing about them was near the top, where we were still standing, these clumps of ten or twelve trees growing close together were held together with a two-foot layer of cement type adhesive. I thought this was odd, but that there must be a reason and that we could look closer as we descended. It would be a long time before we finished the decent; you could only see more and more staircases as you looked through the cracks between them.

Comment: I think this hill, or mountain, is the ministry the Lord has before my husband and I. We have come a long way, and we are in awe that not only are we not yet winded, but even at our ages, we are thriving! Only with God's help could we have undertaken such a climb, but we are still not where we need to be. We have been looking for creative ways to get where we think God wants us to go. The gate indicates the Lord's introduction to a higher more authoritative course.

I look forward to meeting this welcoming couple who will provide for us and facilitate our journey. They may be angels or seasoned ministers themselves. But our arrival at the top, doesn't mean we settle or stay there. The wooden downward staircases and the cement in the pines were all man's creation. My husband and I would descend down the staircases to those in the world who need more of God and His direction. We could appreciate the handiwork, but the beauty and authority was in coming up the steep, green hill on the front side of the house. I never even considered that we would come back up the stairs. To us the stairs were for descending.

This dream also assures us that God has indeed prepared our paths, and it may be that we have some choices yet to make, different winding paths to unknown destinations, but they all lead in the direction He wants us to travel. Each path is just as prepared and securely crafted, and beautiful! Thank you Lord!

Restoration

January 2007: prophetic, provision, angels

I had three dreams last night. I cannot recall the details of the first one, but the second was a repeat of the same theme. Something was being unrighteously stolen from me. The third dream was somehow related, as I was divinely being given something that would somehow cancel the loss.

In the second dream, I saw in front of me a table with a note, like a paycheck, or something representing the like. Also, there were two stacks of money on the table. The money did not look like modern American dollars (nor Israeli shekels). The bills were a larger size, old, and faded but of a dark color, like olive-brown. There were several others around, and we were all making similar types of deposits. Then the dream fast-forwarded to where I was reading the receipt on that deposit. It only recorded the deposit of the note, and no cash. Righteous anger welled up within me; there had been a mistake! A big mistake, as the cash was several times more than the note. I kept seeing the deposit sitting there in my mind, *here is the note for about one thousand, there is the stack of nine thousand, and there is the stack of seven thousand.* I was complaining in the now empty room containing empty tables. Others apparently had similar complaints. The windows closed on us saying the deposits were final. I said something like—what about my seventeen thousand? But it was unheard. *What about these other people who had also been cheated?*

I was walking away, picturing the deposit again in my head and feeling extremely frustrated that there was no proof of that the major part of my deposit had been made. Now I was in arrears, with no hope! I had deposited everything I had. There was nothing more. This was the second dream, so this had happened twice!

Comment: I woke up praying and repenting. I asked God to forgive me for getting so frustrated, as He had taught me that is sin, and I repented of allowing a spirit of frustration to overtake me. I also asked God why I was having frustrating dreams when I specifically prayed as I fell asleep to commune with Him that night. I didn't understand, but I was able to successfully calm my spirit by reciting Psalm 91. Relaxing, I fell asleep again.

I then dreamed the third dream. There was an angel, a small angel who was very childlike and feminine. She had a beautiful face. In fact, she was so close to me that her face was all I could really see of her. First, she was on my right. She was looking up at me and asked, "What is in your mouth?" Suddenly I felt something in my mouth, like two stones—one on either side of my mouth. I spit them into my hand

and found that they were two large cut gemstones of different colors, red and purple. They were much like those I had read about dropping from heaven in Idaho last year—I had been quite skeptical of the reports, as the gemstones I had seen from heaven myself were tiny and of varying shapes.

I was thinking of this as I stared at them for a moment, and then the angel spoke again, "Here."

I looked up to the voice this time, as her head was above me, very close to mine. She opened her mouth and many of these gems poured out of her mouth and into mine. I was trying to catch them all, but my mouth was just not big enough! I said, "Wait..." and I spit them into my two hands as a giant handful. I couldn't believe how many could fit in my mouth.

Again, she spoke, "There's more." I turned and received another mouthful of gems until they were overflowing and slipping out the sides of my mouth. My hands were full, and I couldn't catch them all.

Comment: I woke up feeling that somehow a restoration had taken place. The gems were much like those I had seen from a church in Idaho, fifty millimeters, varying to half that size—but similar and of various colors: red, blue, purple, clear. I also sensed they were symbolic. God had placed something in my mouth that could not be contained. I couldn't close my mouth. I couldn't do anything but let them fall out of my mouth as they had fallen in.

The two piles of undocumented assets in the previous dream, immediately reminded me of transactions that in my recent past had been stolen from me. At the time, the Lord had carefully instructed me not to defend myself and not to make demands. One of those times the Lord said, "Vengeance is mine—I will repay." My reaction in the dream of frustration was much less intense than what I had been through in the past few years regarding these types of unjust transactions.

I also had the sense that this was a second dream on the same topic—something had been stolen and not recovered. In fact, I have had several experiences in my life that have happened in pairs when something has been stolen. The two stones meant restoration to me, but it wasn't because of the value of the stones, versus the value of the transactions. I believe it is the feeling of victimization when injustice touches your life. The feeling of being a victim was replaced by heavenly power, authority, and provision in the form of these gemstones I received. These things the enemy has no power to take away.

I looked up the meanings of the colors of the stones and received a friend's suggestions. Red can signify the Blood of Jesus and victory in this case. Purple or blue/red can speak of a heavenly covering, as the veil in the temple dividing the priestly service area from the Holiest of Holies. This might mean that God is indeed declaring divine intervention regarding restoration. Another interpretation could be, red is the color of royalty, and purple/amethyst a color of sobriety—in the office of a bishop or apostle. If the dream is speaking of the old or ancient robbery from my family line and all through my life, this could mean not only a restoration and moving forward into receiving financial abundance but also abundance in revelation and the authority to bring light to the falsehoods and unjust transactions. It could also signify a calling on my life in the office of priest, apostle, or bishop to clarify confusing and heretical doctrine. I believe all of these are indicated to some extent.

I understand the stones to represent not only the divine words and messages but also delivery in a divine way. I have been praying for the gift of understanding and speaking various languages. A gift of communication, I call it. It isn't that I want to be one who just masters many languages, but rather that I desire to be one who is understood by all. This would be considered a sign and a wonder—not my intellect.

The angel was not like any I had ever seen. In fact, I never notice their faces, instead I usually notice their garments. I didn't see her garment at all. I have never encountered a feminine angel before either. I don't know if the details of her face are significant, but this is how I would describe it: She had a small childlike face with extremely large bright eyes. They were a color difficult to describe. They were like the colors of the ocean, from blue to green to purple, but they were light colored and clear like the sky. I also saw some wisps of yellow wavy hair framing her face. Again, the yellow was more like gold. Her complexion was also light and somewhat translucent. I believe this angel represents the Holy Spirit, the one who puts the words in my mouth that I might speak the oracles of God.

I don't know for certain what it is that God wants to use me to communicate, but I want to cooperate! *Use me Lord! Father God, I give you my mouth, my mind, my life. Use me as You choose, in Jesus Name!*

A Song from the Day You Were Formed

January 2007: prophetic

> Every one that is called by my name: I have created for my glory, I have formed him; yea, I have made him.
>
> Isaiah 43:7

I was hurrying to get ready for my turn. There were angelic guides looking very much like ordinary people, and they were directing us to dress and prepare. When they told me I would be expected to dance as I sang the song from the day I was formed, my heart was both ecstatic and fearful. The thought of the song made my heart leap—but I am not a singer. Could I recall the words? It had been a very long time since I heard them. Moreover, I am even less of a dancer; *klutz* was the word I used to describe my level of gracefulness on earth. Could I possibly know what moves to make and remember the words at the same time? As if the angels could hear my thoughts, they assured me that the words would appear on the wall—not to worry.

After I was dressed and prepared, we walked down a hall and came to a door. I entered the room where I would share my song and dance. My clothing surprised me, as it was a camouflage blend of colors—very earthy, but thin and transparent—wispy. Somehow, I knew it was correct though. The room was tiered with a light blue carpet and could hold only about fifty people standing and sitting. There were a number of people and angels, but it wasn't full. I'm not sure how I could tell them apart—but I could. In the center of the room was an open area where the people would take their turn and share. A woman was doing her dance as I walked in. She had short brown hair, she also wasn't physically graceful and I could only see her mouthing the words—not really singing, sort of saying the words, but it was simplistically beautiful. She pantomimed God speaking over her and then looked up and around as if she was looking for the reaction of a heavenly cloud of witnesses. My eye caught on the words on the wall. I was surprised to see them in script, a kind of cursive print that could have been English. This reassured me that if I forgot words there would be a reminder over my shoulder. I moved in to kneel down to start my dance.

> I will praise thee; for I am fearfully and wonderfully made: marvelous are thy works; and that my soul knows right well. My substance was not hid from thee, when I was made in secret, and curiously wrought in the lowest parts of the earth. Thine eyes did see my substance, yet being unformed; and in thy book all my members were written, which in continuance were fashioned, when as yet there was none of them.
>
> Psalm 139:4–16

Comment: This dream amazes me. The fact that I was fully aware in the dream that such a song exists, amazes me even now. I have never thought about the day I was formed. I cannot imagine how many eons ago this may have been. This was not the day I was born, nor the day I was conceived—but the day the Lord took thought of me—who I would be, my personality, my physical design, my spiritual being—the *real* me. In my heart I knew the song, I would recognize it as the angel played the tune, I would know what movements went with it, and the Lord would bring the words back *if* I was simply worshipping Him and not concerned about *me*. My overall feelings during the dream were of loving humility and obedience.

The color blue of the carpet reminds me of the heavenly place I was in. The transparent green and brown of my garment speak of my earthiness and my prophetic tendencies to see and operate in the spiritual realm. I only saw the sleeve on my arm—I have no idea what the rest of me looked like. I find the details of this dream very difficult to describe. Even now as I recall this dream, I am overcome with His thoughts for me—His joy in creating me for His divine purpose.

In the dance, I began by sitting on my feet on the floor, looking down. My arms were down with my hands touching the floor. My head also was looking toward the floor. I understood that I would quickly rise up, my arms and head lifted to the heavens as I stood. Then I would blossom as a flower. All of this event's sequence was in my head, though I didn't know how I was going to act it through. I just *knew* the creative, divine music would trigger my body to respond. I was not only willing, but I trembled with enthusiasm and excitement to participate.

Dream Interpretation & References

There have been many books written on the subject of dreams and dream interpretation over the years. Many of them are not from a Biblical perspective. I have referenced a couple of Christian resources concerning my own dreams. They are included at the end of this chapter. I have also attended a couple conferences through my church. The Bible only mentions Joseph and Daniel as having the gift of interpreting dreams. The Holy Spirit is our best guide. Accountable Christian mentors and friends can pray with you to help determine what God is saying.

No one book will have all the answers. There is no single meaning to what may appear in your dreams. There are typical meanings for colors, numbers, things or situations but your own experiences shape the meanings. The most important understanding is what the dream means to you personally. Input from others can be helpful, but all opinions must witness to you and be confirmed by the Holy Spirit. Every prophecy, dream, or vision must be tested against the Word of God. God always confirms what He is saying.

Not all dreams are from God. No one besides the Holy Spirit has the complete understanding of your dream. The thing to remember is that God does speak to us in dreams and visions. Usually it is about us, sometimes about our families, and on rare occasions, it may be a message from God to a larger audience. Dreams and visions can be about circumstances in our past, our lives right now or they may look forward toward things to come. Just as certain scriptures in the Bible can have relevance to the day when they were written about and also look forward to a future event, so also with our dreams sometimes. God may simply be giving you revelation about His character, or your own, so that you can have a closer relationship with Him.

There are simple instructions for hearing God speak to you in dreams and visions. First of all, ask God to speak to you and give you ears to hear and eyes to see so that you may understand. Then when you do have a dream or vision, write it down. You may remember more at a later time and add to it. But it is good to write it when it is fresh in your mind. Once you write it down, ask God for the meaning. Then prayerfully wait and listen—meditate on what God is trying to communicate to you. Sometimes it takes days or years for the understanding to come. Other times it will be quickly. Sometimes an event happens in your life and you suddenly realize that was the meaning of the dream. Or you may be reading a portion of Scripture and suddenly the dream fits, and your understanding is enlightened to what God was trying to explain.

If you know a dream is from the Lord, pray into it. Dreams from God should not cause us to fear, rather to pray for His Will in every situation. It is also wise to go to someone accountable whom you respect to get advice and discernment about some dreams. Not every pastor or leader will be supportive. You can trust God, that if He is speaking to you and you are seeking Him, He will direct you in discovering keys to unlock the meanings.

Dreams and visions from God are scriptural. As you read the example Scripture references below, notice how some give direction or teaching and some are prophetic. The Lord will also use dreams to help us endure the trials and tests that may be ahead of us. We live in the Last Days, according to Scripture. This is a spiritual season of increased dreams and visions. Expect God to speak to you, even if this is new to you and you have never dreamed or remembered your dreams before.

> Call unto me, and I will answer thee, and shew thee great and mighty things, which thou knowest not.
>
> Jeremiah 33:3

Scriptural References

Now a thing was secretly brought to me, and mine ear received a little thereof. In thoughts from the visions of the night, when deep sleep falleth on men ...

Job 4:13

And the LORD answered me, and said, Write the vision, and make it plain upon tables, that he may run that readeth it. For the vision is yet for an appointed time, but at the end it shall speak, and not lie: though it tarry, wait for it; because it will surely come, it will not tarry.

Habakkuk 2:2–3

But God came to Abimelech in a dream by night, and said to him, Behold, thou art but a dead man, for the woman which thou hast taken; for she is a man's wife. But Abimelech had not come near her: and he said, Lord, wilt thou slay also a righteous nation? Said he not unto me, She is my sister? and she, even she herself said, He is my brother: in the integrity of my heart and

> innocency of my hands have I done this. And God said unto him in a dream, Yea, I know that thou didst this in the integrity of thy heart; for I also withheld thee from sinning against me: therefore suffered I thee not to touch her. Now therefore restore the man his wife; for he is a prophet, and he shall pray for thee, and thou shalt live: and if thou restore her not, know thou that thou shalt surely die, thou, and all that are thine.
>
> Genesis 20:3–7

Genesis 28:11–17: Dream of Jacob, concerning the ladder to heaven and God's promise of blessing

Genesis 37:5–10: Dream of Joseph, concerning the sheaves and the sun, moon and stars. This prophetic dream showed Joseph what was to come. The interpretation was obvious.

Genesis 40:8–19: Dreams of the butler and baker interpreted by Joseph.

Genesis 41:1–36: Dream of Pharaoh was a warning from God to Pharaoh about the famine, only Joseph could interpret.

> And God spake unto Israel in the visions of the night, and said, Jacob, Jacob. And he said, Here am I. And he said, I am God, the God of thy father: fear not to go down into Egypt; for I will there make of thee a great nation: I will go down with thee into Egypt; and I will also surely bring thee up again: and Joseph shall put his hand upon thine eyes.
>
> Genesis 46:2–4

1 Kings 3:5–15: Dream of Solomon, he chose wisdom as the gift from God and God promises to bless him with much more.

Daniel: 2: Dream of King Nebuchadnezzar about future kingdoms; only Daniel can interpret.

Daniel 4:1–27 Dream of King Nebuchadnezzar becoming a beast; only Daniel can interpret.

Daniel 7: Daniel's prophetic dream of the four beasts.

> And it shall come to pass afterward, that I will pour out my spirit upon all flesh; and your sons and your daughters shall prophesy, your old men shall dream dreams, your young men shall see visions: And also upon the servants and upon the handmaids in those days will I pour out my spirit.
>
> Joel 2:28, 29

Published References

- *Dream Language: The Prophetic Power of Dreams* by James W. and Michal Ann Goll

- *The Prophet's Dictionary: The Ultimate Guide to Supernatural Wisdom* by Paula A., Ph.D. Price

- *Exploring the World of Dreams* by Denny Thomas

- *Understanding the Dreams you Dream* by Ira Milligan

- *Dreams and Visions* by Jane Hamon

- *Dancing With Destiny: Awaken your Heart to Dream, to Love, to War* by Jill Austin

For this cause I bow my knees unto the Father of our Lord Jesus Christ, of whom the whole family in heaven and earth is named, that he would grant you, according to the riches of his glory, to be strengthened with might by his Spirit in the inner man; that Christ may dwell in your hearts by faith; that ye, being rooted and grounded in love, may be able to comprehend with all saints what is the breadth, and length, and depth, and height; and to know the love of Christ, which passeth knowledge, that ye might be filled with all the fullness of God. Now unto him that is able to do exceeding abundantly above all that we ask or think, according to the power that worketh in us, unto him be glory in the church by Christ Jesus throughout all ages, world without end. Amen.

Ephesians 3:14–21

Index of Dream Categories

Airplane 64, 91, 168, 177
Angels 111, 155, 222
End Times. 51, 72, 97, 103, 108, 117, 121, 164, 168, 177
Heaven 60, 69, 75, 83, 87, 91, 100, 114, 117, 158
Houses 22, 148, 205, 212, 219,
Prophetic. . . 28, 33, 35, 38, 54, 69, 89, 94, 100, 111, 121, 123, 130, 138, 142, 155, 158, 162, 173, 185, 190, 193, 197, 201, 205, 209, 219, 222, 227
Provision 38, 54, 144, 151, 170, 190, 201, 222
Servants 148, 160, 190
Spiritual Warfare 20, 25, 30, 41, 51, 57, 78, 105, 108, 127, 135, 197
Vision 160
Vision of God 17, 44, 66, 180

Endnotes

1. The Voice of the Martyrs www.persecution.com
2. The Persecuted Church www.persecutedchurch.org